Mastercam Exercises

Published by
CADIN360
cadin360.com
Copyright © 2019 by CADIN360, All rights reserved.

Limit of Liability/Disclaimer of Warranty:

Examination Copies

Electronic Files

Disclaimer:

Preface

Mastercam Exercises

❖ This book contain 200 CAD practice exercises and drawings.

❖ This book does not provide step by step tutorial to design 3D models.

❖ S.I Unit is used.

❖ Predominantly used Third Angle Projection.

❖ This book is for **Mastercam** and Other Feature-Based Modeling Software such as Inventor, SolidWorks, NX, Solid Edge, AutoCAD, PTC Creo etc.

❖ It is intended to provide Drafters, Designers and Engineers with enough 3D CAD exercises for practice on **Mastercam**.

❖ It includes almost all types of exercises that are necessary to provide, clear, concise and systematic information required on industrial machine part drawings.

❖ Third Angle Projection is intentionally used to familiarize Drafters, Designers and Engineers in Third Angle Projection to meet the expectation of world wide Engineering drawing print.

❖ Clear and well drafted drawing help easy understanding of the design.

❖ This book is for Beginner, Intermediate and Advance CAD users.

❖ These exercises are from Basics to Advance level.

❖ Each exercises can be assigned and designed separately.

❖ No Exercise is a prerequisite for another. All dimensions are in mm.

❖ Note: Assume any missing dimensions.

EX-01

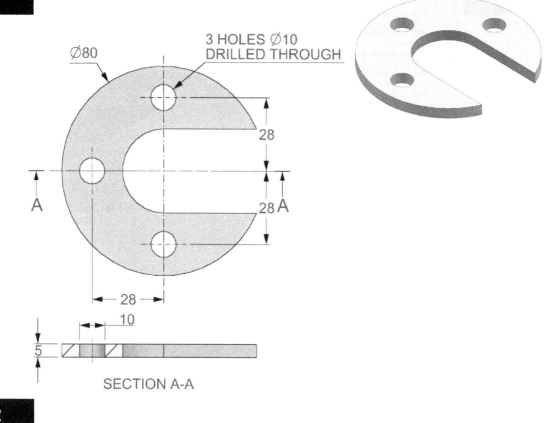

Ø80

3 HOLES Ø10
DRILLED THROUGH

28

28

A

28 A

28

10

5

SECTION A-A

EX-02

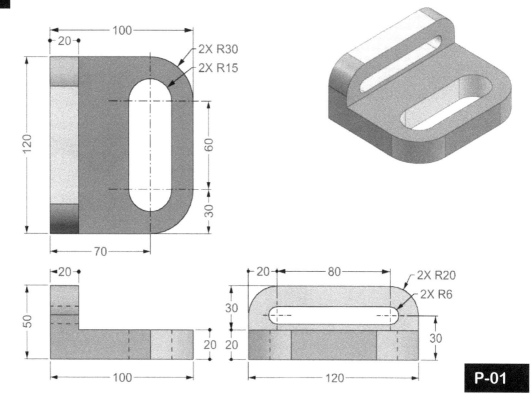

100

20

2X R30

2X R15

120

60

30

70

20

50

100

20

20

20

80

2X R20

2X R6

30

30

120

P-01

EX-03

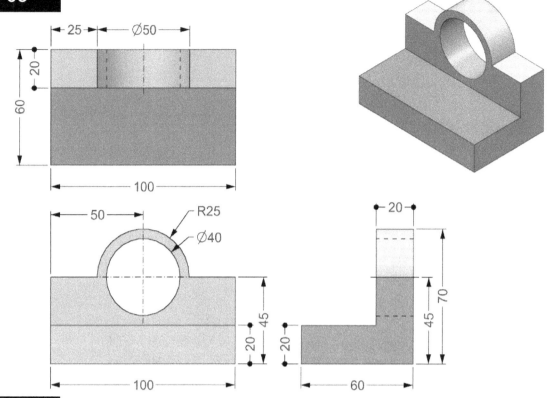

- 25
- Ø50
- 20
- 60
- 100

- 50
- R25
- Ø40
- 45
- 20
- 100

- 20
- 70
- 45
- 20
- 60

EX-04

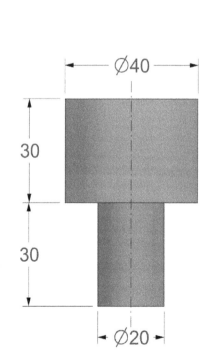

- Ø40
- 30
- 30
- Ø20

EX-05

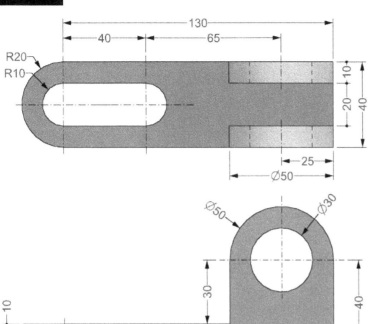
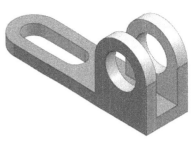
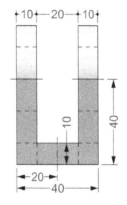

EX-06

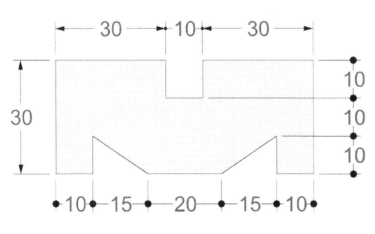
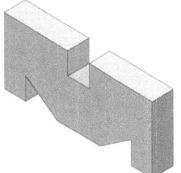
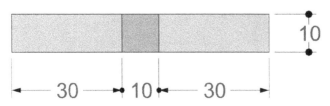

EX-07

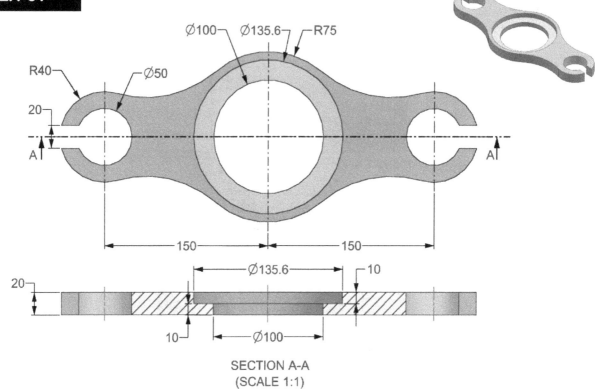

Ø100 Ø135.6 R75
R40 Ø50
20
A
150 150
A

20
Ø135.6 10
10 Ø100

SECTION A-A
(SCALE 1:1)

EX-08

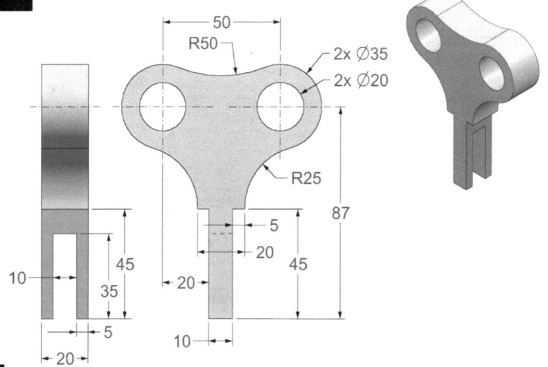

50
R50
2x Ø35
2x Ø20
R25
87
45
10 45
10 35
20 5
5 20
10
20

P-04

EX-09

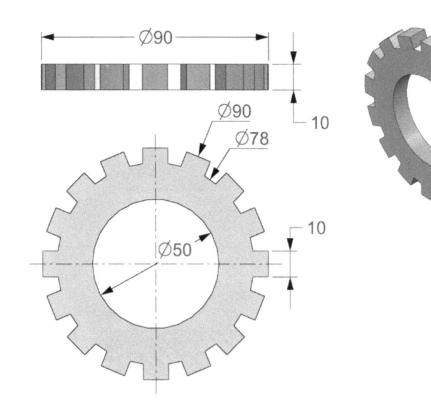

⌀90

10

⌀90
⌀78
⌀50

10

EX-10

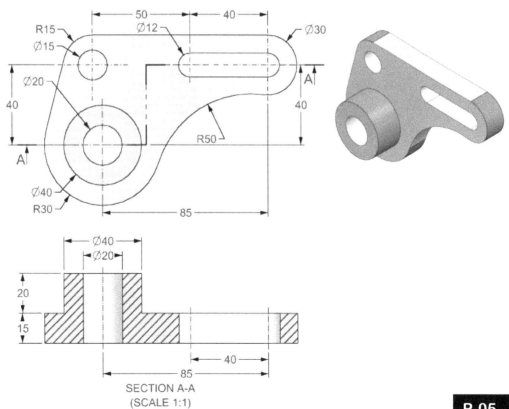

50
40
R15
⌀12
⌀30
⌀15
A
⌀20
40
40
R50
R30
⌀40
85

⌀40
⌀20
20
15
40
85

SECTION A-A
(SCALE 1:1)

P-05

EX-11

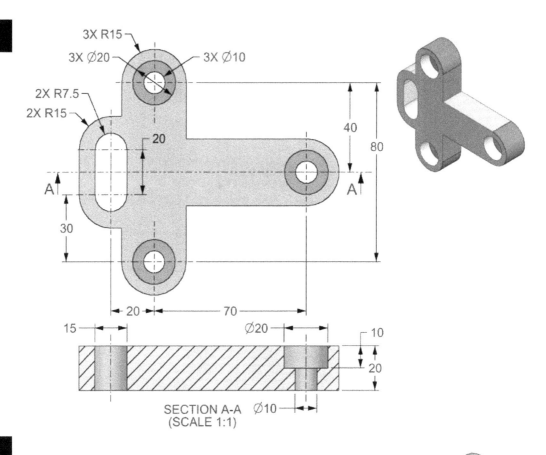

3X R15
3X Ø20
3X Ø10
2X R7.5
2X R15
20
40
80
A
A
30
20
70

15
Ø20
10
20
Ø10

SECTION A-A
(SCALE 1:1)

EX-12

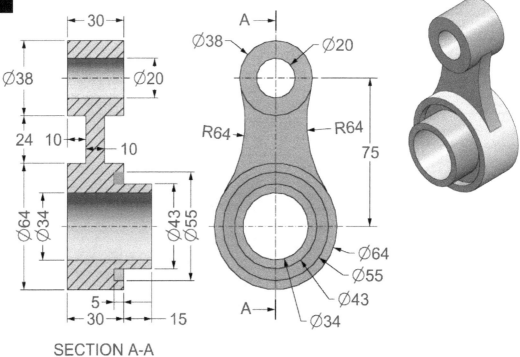

30
Ø38
Ø20
24   10
10
Ø64
Ø34
Ø43
Ø55
5
30
15

A
Ø38
Ø20
R64
R64
75
Ø64
Ø55
Ø43
A
Ø34

SECTION A-A
(SCALE 1:1)

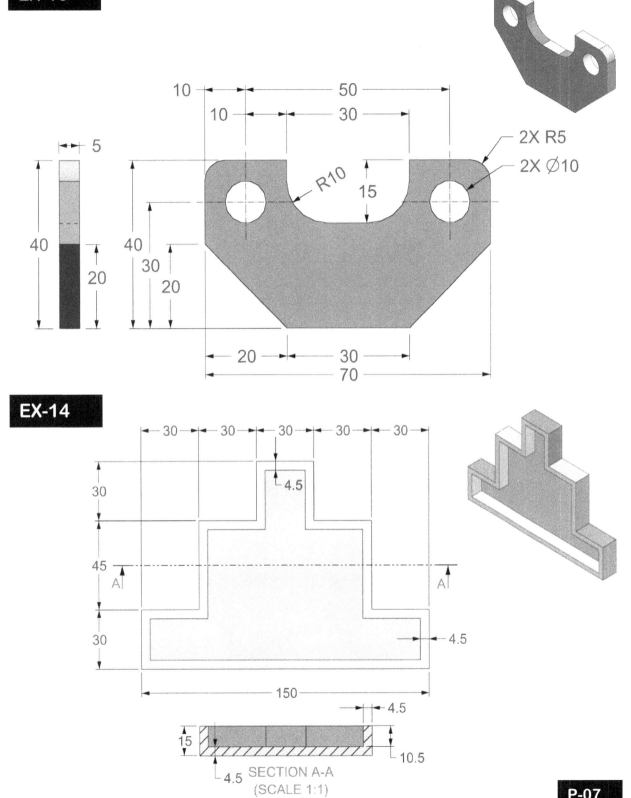

EX-13

10
50
10
30
2X R5
2X Ø10
R10
15
5
40
40
30
20
20
20
30
70

EX-14

30 30 30 30 30
30
4.5
45
A
A
30
4.5
150
4.5
15
10.5
4.5
SECTION A-A
(SCALE 1:1)

P-07

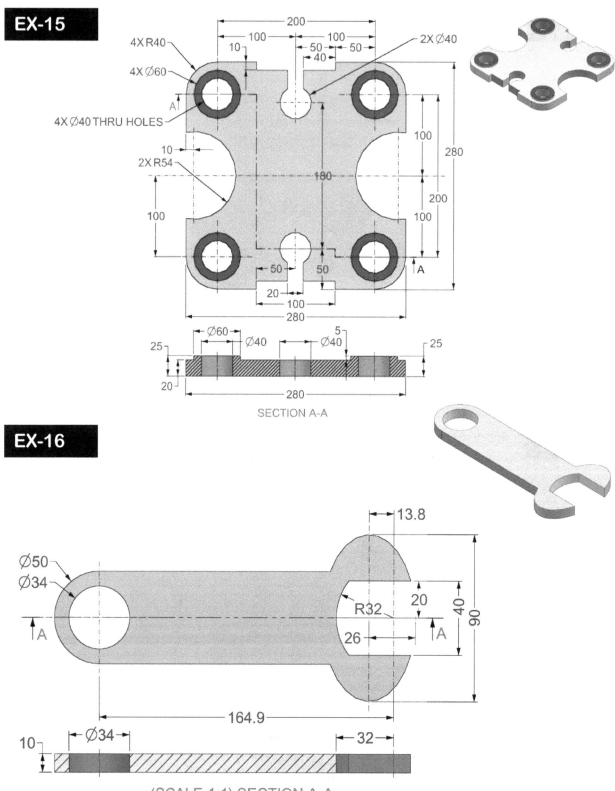

EX-15

4X R40
4X Ø60
4X Ø40 THRU HOLES
2X R54
2X Ø40

200
100
100
10
50
50
40
10
180
100
280
200
100
100
50
50
20
100
280

A

Ø60
Ø40
5
Ø40
25
25
20
280

SECTION A-A

EX-16

Ø50
Ø34
13.8
20
40
90
R32
26
A
164.9

Ø34
10
32

(SCALE 1:1) SECTION A-A

P-08

EX-17

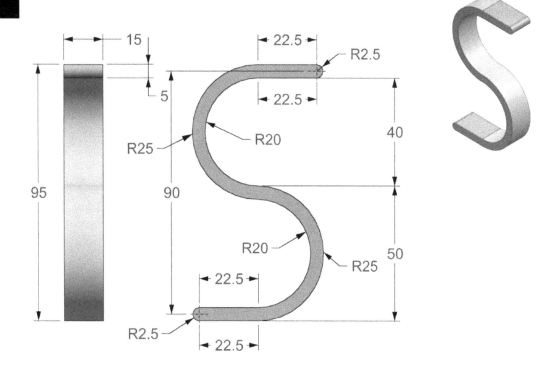

15

22.5 — R2.5

5

22.5

R25 — R20

40

95

90

R20 — R25

50

R2.5

22.5

22.5

EX-18

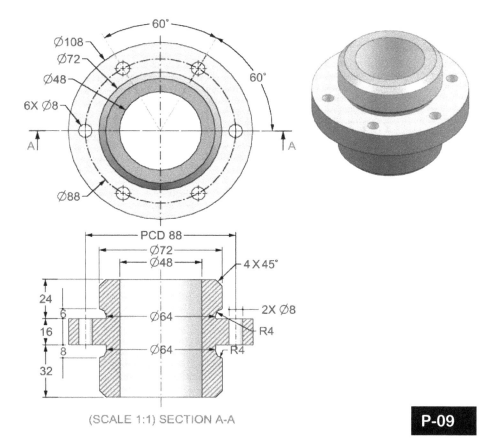

60°

Ø108
Ø72
Ø48

6X Ø8

60°

A — A

Ø88

PCD 88
Ø72
Ø48

4 X 45°

24

6

Ø64

2X Ø8

16

Ø64

R4

8

Ø64

R4

32

(SCALE 1:1) SECTION A-A

P-09

EX-19

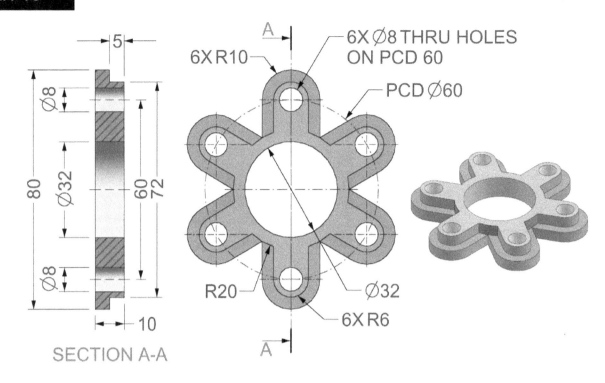

6X R10
6X Ø8 THRU HOLES ON PCD 60
PCD Ø60
Ø32
6X R6
R20

Ø8
Ø32
80
60
72
Ø8
5
10

SECTION A-A

EX-20

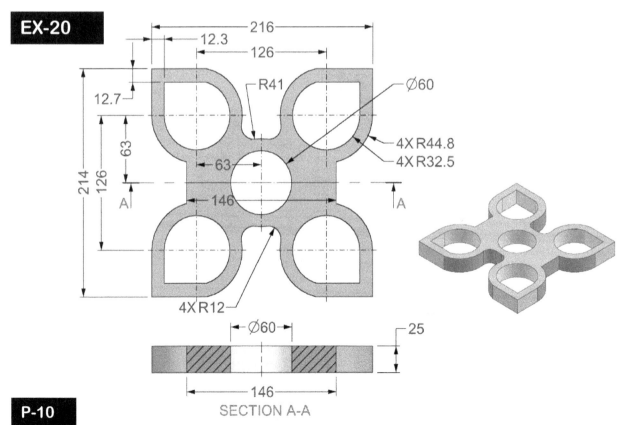

216
12.3
126
R41
Ø60
12.7
63
63
146
4X R44.8
4X R32.5
214
126
4X R12

Ø60
25
146

SECTION A-A

EX-21

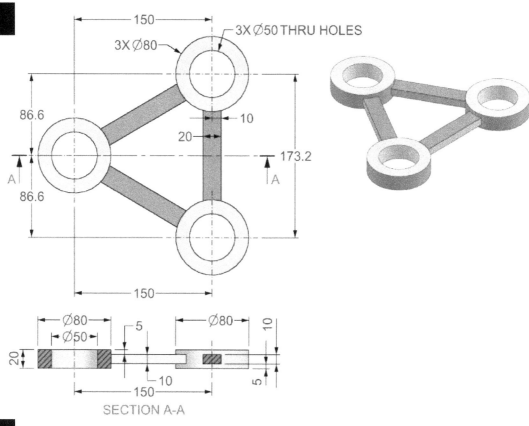

150

3X Ø50 THRU HOLES

3X Ø80

86.6

10

20

173.2

A

A

86.6

150

Ø80

Ø50

20

5

Ø80

10

10

5

150

SECTION A-A

EX-22

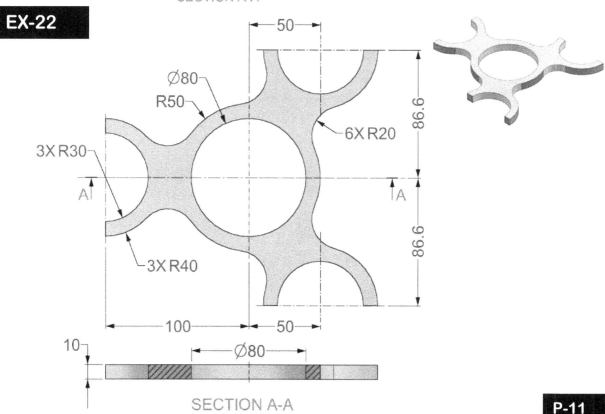

50

Ø80

R50

86.6

6X R20

3X R30

A

A

86.6

3X R40

100

50

10

Ø80

SECTION A-A

P-11

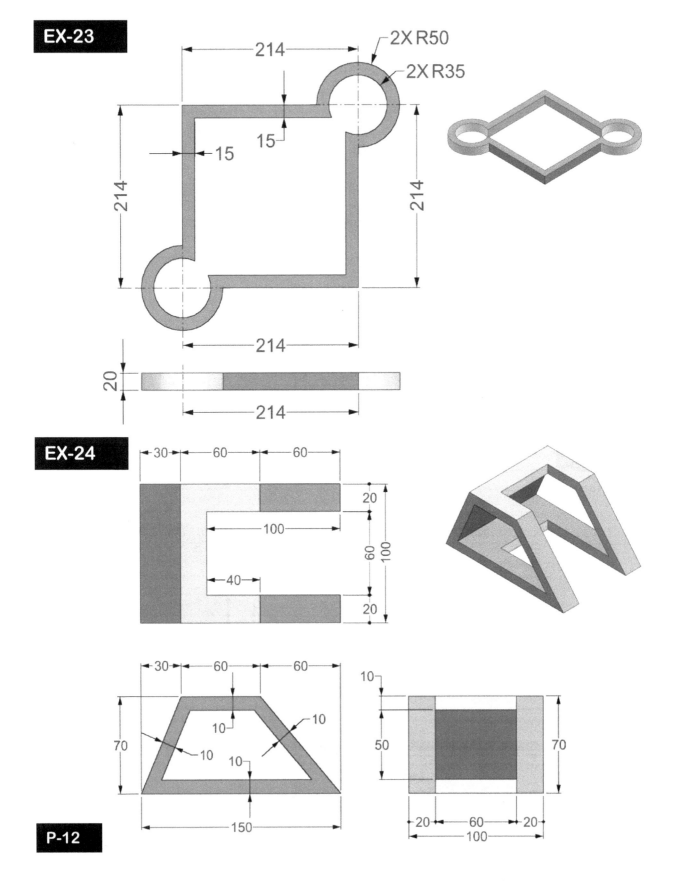

EX-23

2X R50
2X R35
214
15
15
214
214
214
20
214

EX-24

30
60
60
20
100
60
100
40
20

P-12

30
60
60
10
10
10
10
70
10
150

10
50
70
20
60
20
100

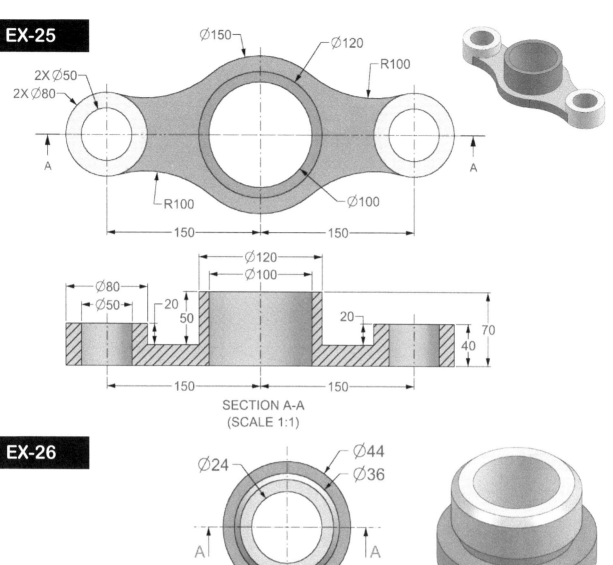

EX-25

Ø150 Ø120 R100
2X Ø50 2X Ø80
R100 Ø100
150 150

Ø80 Ø120
Ø50 Ø100
20 50 20 70 40
150 150

SECTION A-A
(SCALE 1:1)

EX-26

Ø24 Ø44 Ø36
A A

Ø44 Ø36 Ø32 Ø24 2X45°
12 8 36 12
4 3

SECTION A-A
(SCALE 1:1)

EX-27

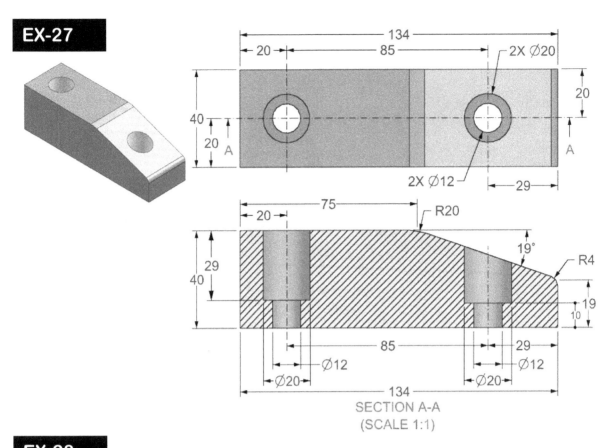

134
20
85
2X Ø20
20
40
20
A
A
2X Ø12
29

75
R20
20
19°
R4
29
40
19
10
85
29
Ø12
Ø12
Ø20
Ø20
134
SECTION A-A
(SCALE 1:1)

EX-28

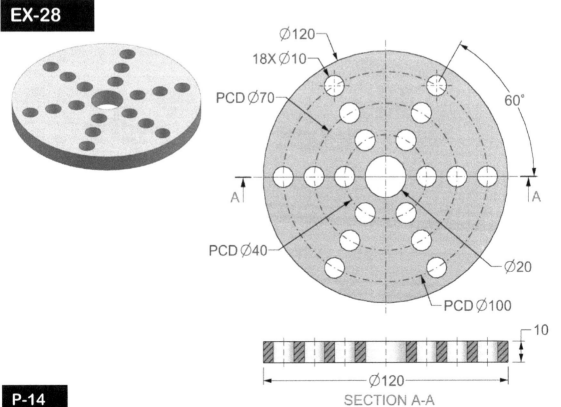

Ø120
18X Ø10
60°
PCD Ø70
PCD Ø40
Ø20
A
A
PCD Ø100
10
Ø120
SECTION A-A

P-14

EX-29

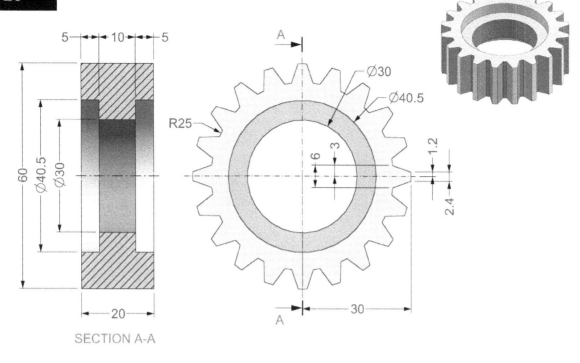

SECTION A-A

5 | 10 | 5
60
Ø40.5
Ø30
20

A
A
Ø30
Ø40.5
R25
6
3
1.2
2.4
30

EX-30

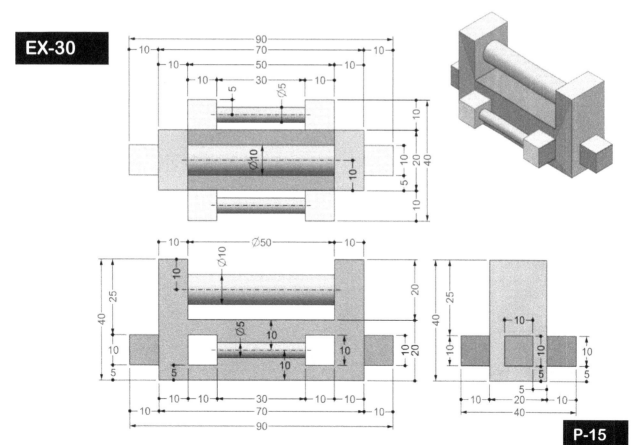

90
10 | 70 | 10
10 | 50 | 10
10 | 30 | 10
5
Ø5
10
40
20
10
5
10

Ø50
Ø10
10
10
40
25
10
5
Ø5
10
20
20
10
10
10 | 10 | 30 | 10 | 10
10 | 70 | 10
90

40
25
10
5
10
10
10
5
5
10 | 20 | 10
40

P-15

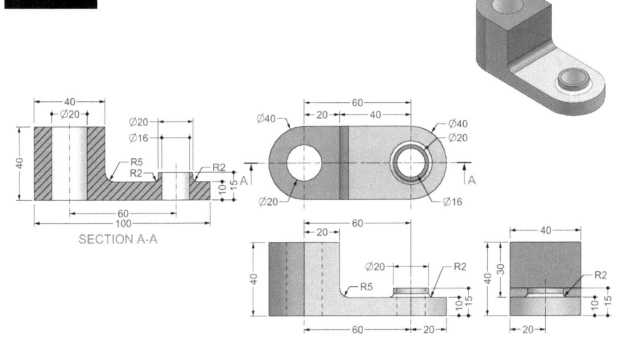

SECTION A-A

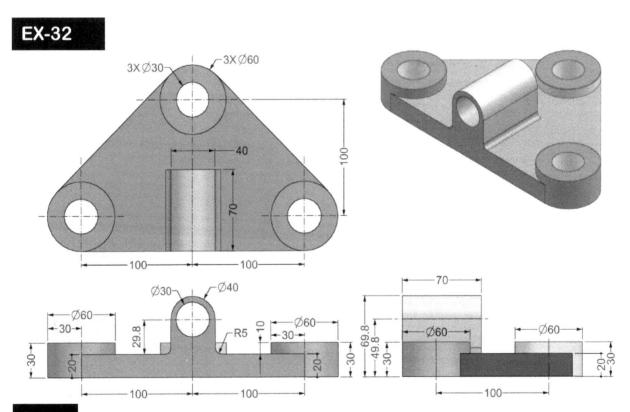

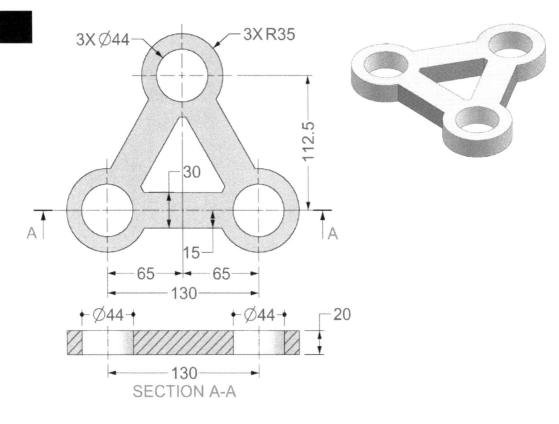

3X ⌀44
3X R35
112.5
30
15
65
65
130
A
A
⌀44
⌀44
20
130
SECTION A-A

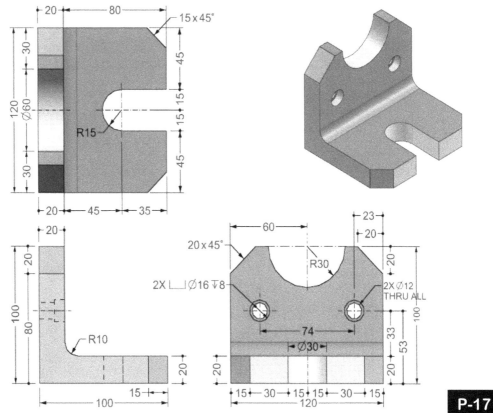

20
80
15 x 45°
30
45
120
⌀60
15 15
15
R15
45
30
20
45
35

20
20
100
80
R10
20
15

60
23
20
20 x 45°
R30
2X ⌀16 ▼8
2X ⌀12 THRU ALL
74
100
⌀30
33
53
20
20
15 30 15 15 30 15
120

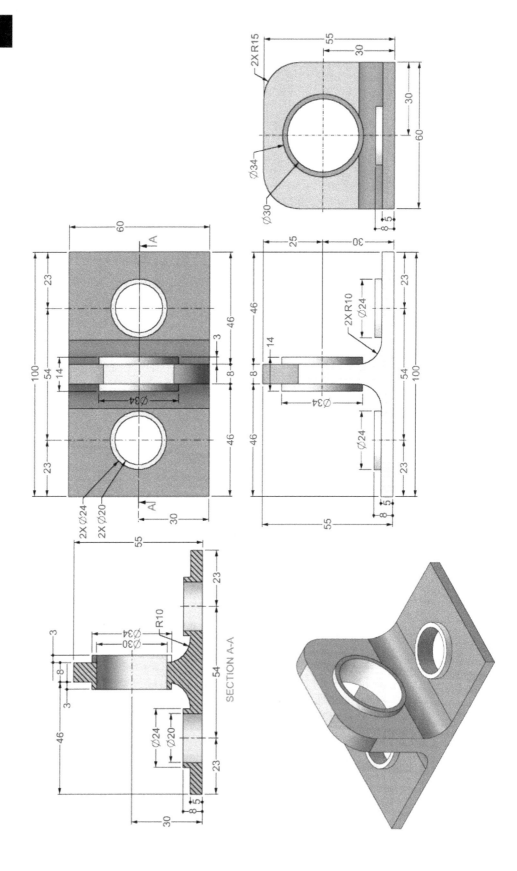

2X R15

55

30

30

60

Ø34

Ø30

8
5

60

A

23

46

3

100

54

14

8

Ø34

46

23

A

30

2X Ø24

2X Ø20

25

30

46

14

2X R10

Ø24

23

8

Ø34

54

100

46

Ø24

23

8
5

55

55

23

3

Ø34
Ø30

R10

8

3

54

46

Ø24
Ø20

23

8
5

30

SECTION A-A

EX-36

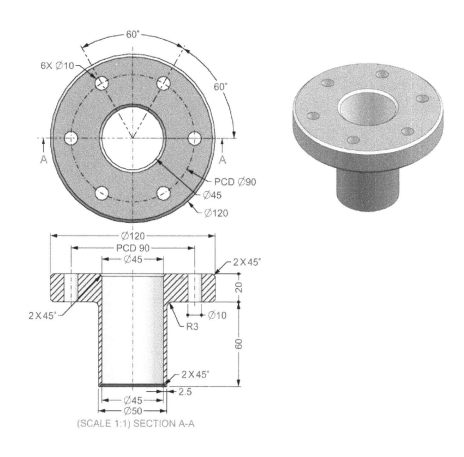

60°
6X Ø10
60°
A — A
PCD Ø90
Ø45
Ø120

Ø120
PCD 90
Ø45
2 X 45°
20
2 X 45°
Ø10
R3
60
2 X 45°
2.5
Ø45
Ø50
(SCALE 1:1) SECTION A-A

EX-37

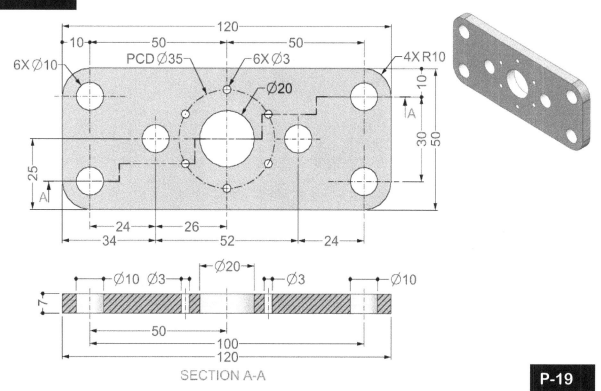

120
10
50
50
6X Ø10
PCD Ø35
6X Ø3
4X R10
Ø20
10
A
30
50
25
A
24
26
34
52
24

Ø20
Ø10 Ø3
Ø3
Ø10
7
50
100
120
SECTION A-A

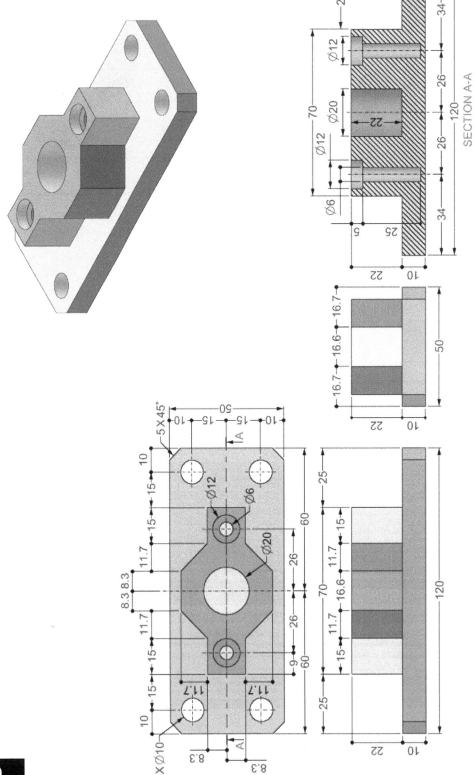

SECTION A-A

EX-39

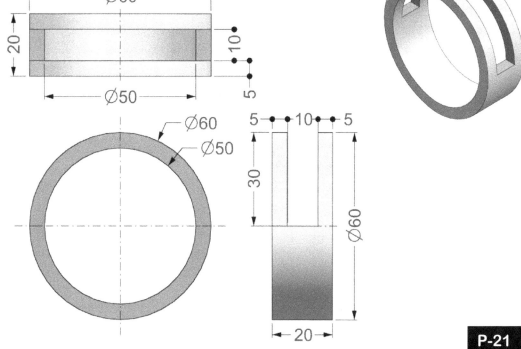

70
R20
Ø20
40
45

R25
Ø20
45
10
20
30
10
A
A
45
65

20
2X R10
Ø40
Ø20
25
45
SECTION A-A

EX-40

Ø60
20
10
5
Ø50

Ø60
Ø50

5
10
5
30
Ø60
20

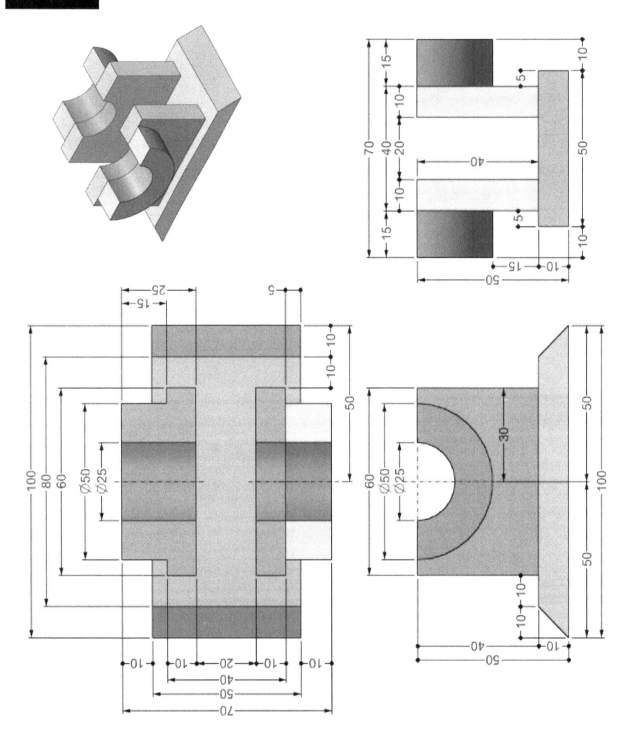

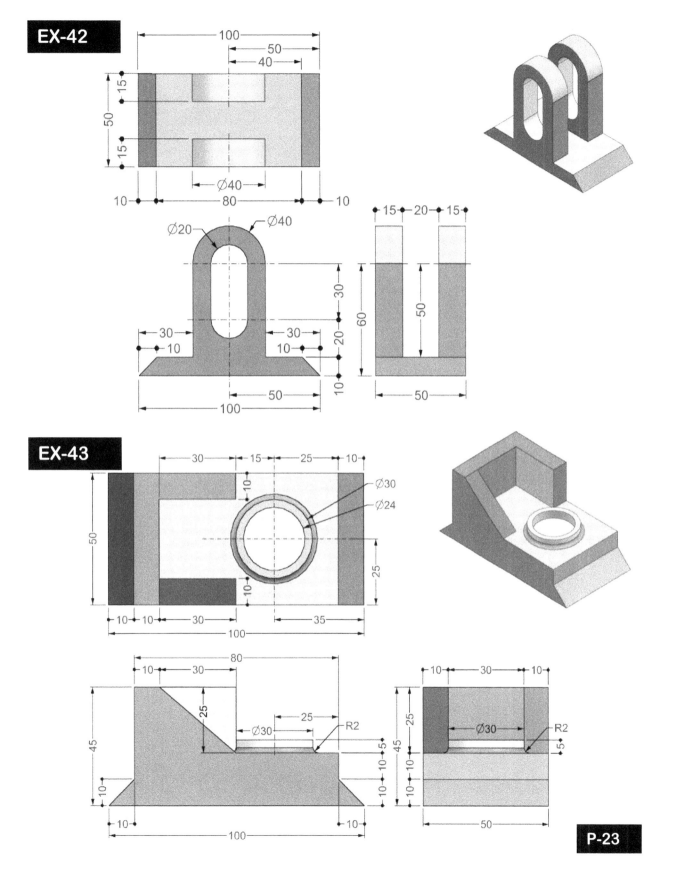

EX-42

EX-43

P-23

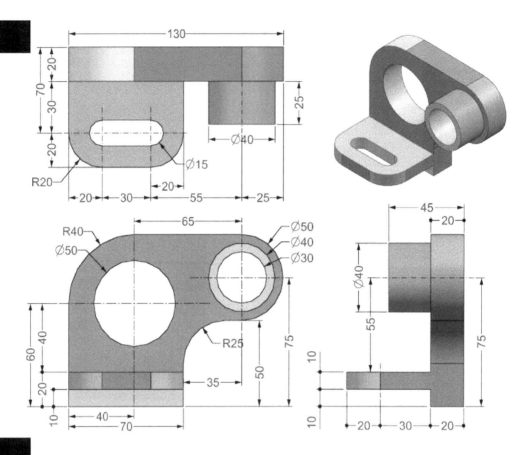

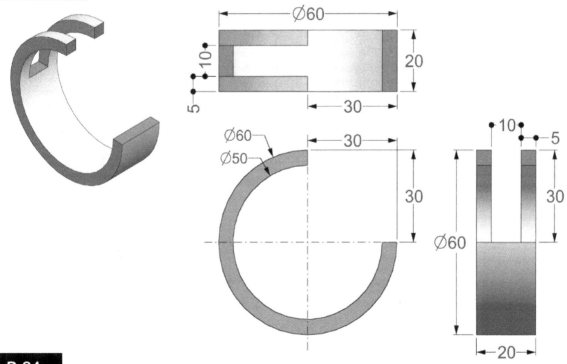

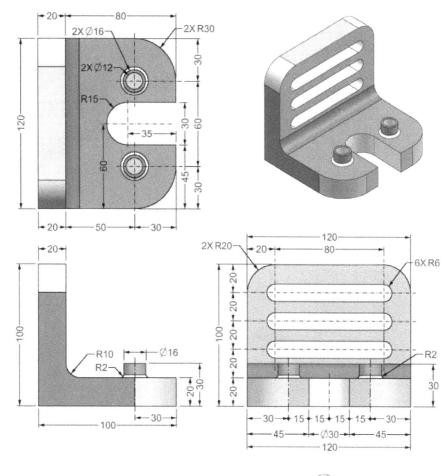

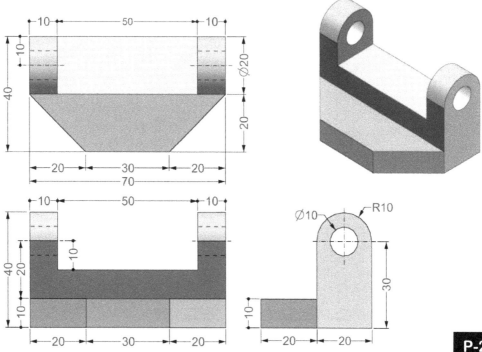

EX-48

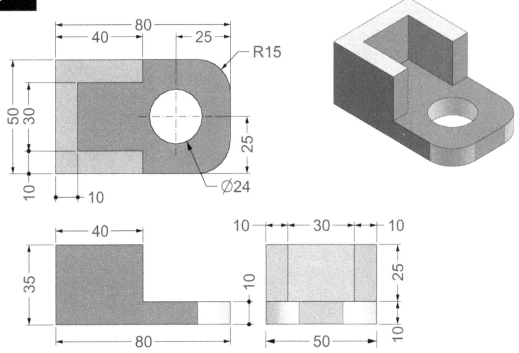

EX-49

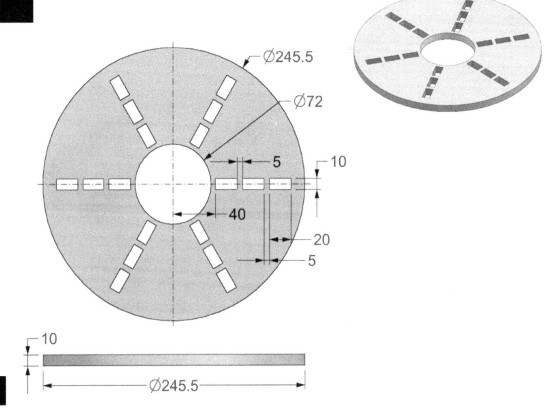

P-26

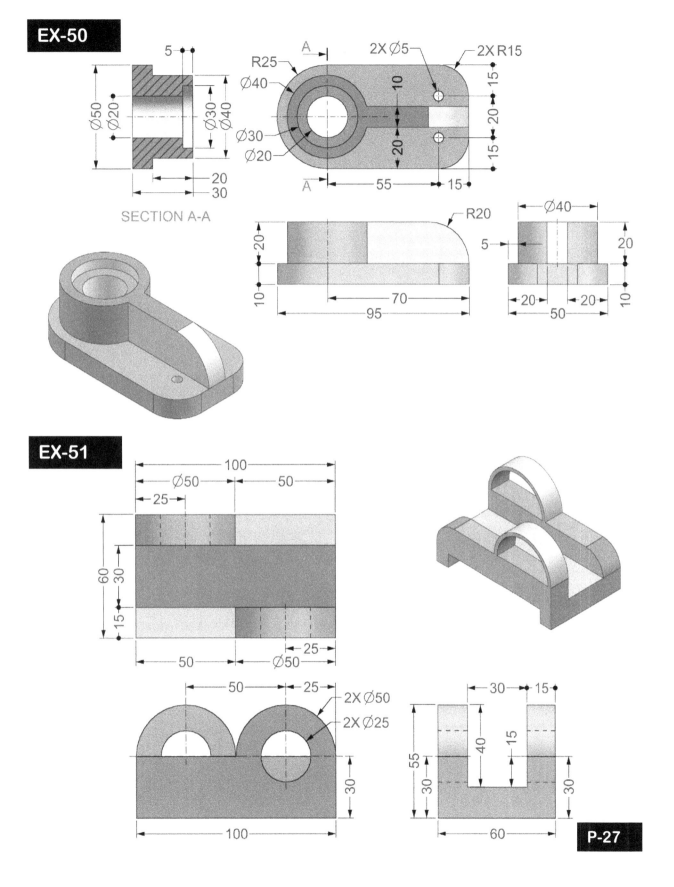

EX-50

5
Ø50
Ø20
Ø30
Ø40
20
30

SECTION A-A

A
R25
Ø40
Ø30
Ø20
2X Ø5
2X R15
10
15
20
15
20
15
55
15
A

R20
20
10
70
95

Ø40
5
20
20
20
50
10

EX-51

100
Ø50
50
25
60
30
15
50
Ø50
25

50
25
2X Ø50
2X Ø25
30
100

30
15
55
40
15
30
30
60

P-27

EX-52

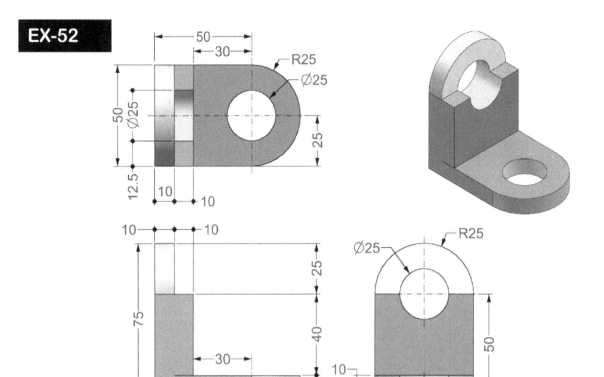

EX-53

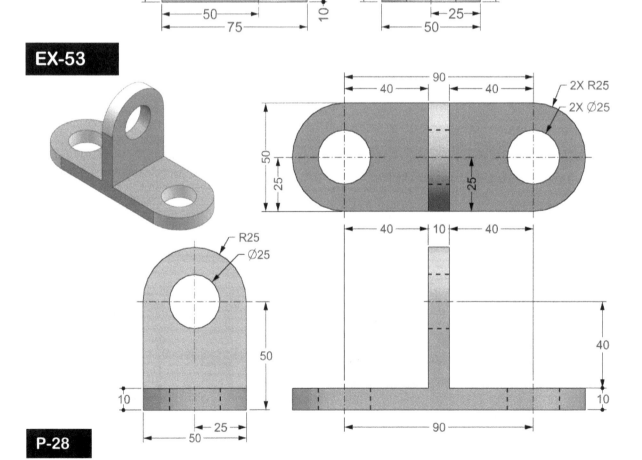

EX-54

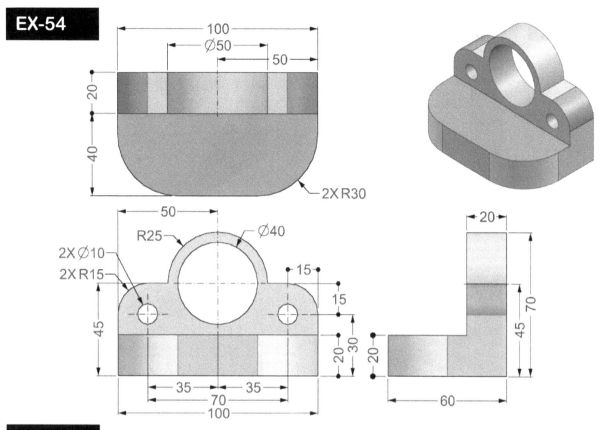

100
Ø50
50
20
40
2X R30

50
R25
Ø40
2X Ø10
2X R15
15
15
45
20
30
35
35
70
100
20
70
45
20
60

EX-55

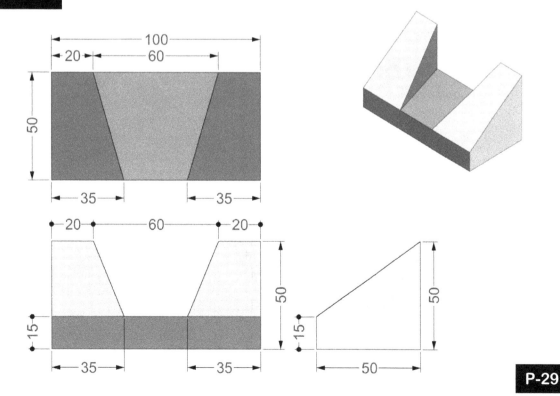

100
20
60
50
35
35

20
60
20
50
15
35
35

50
15
50

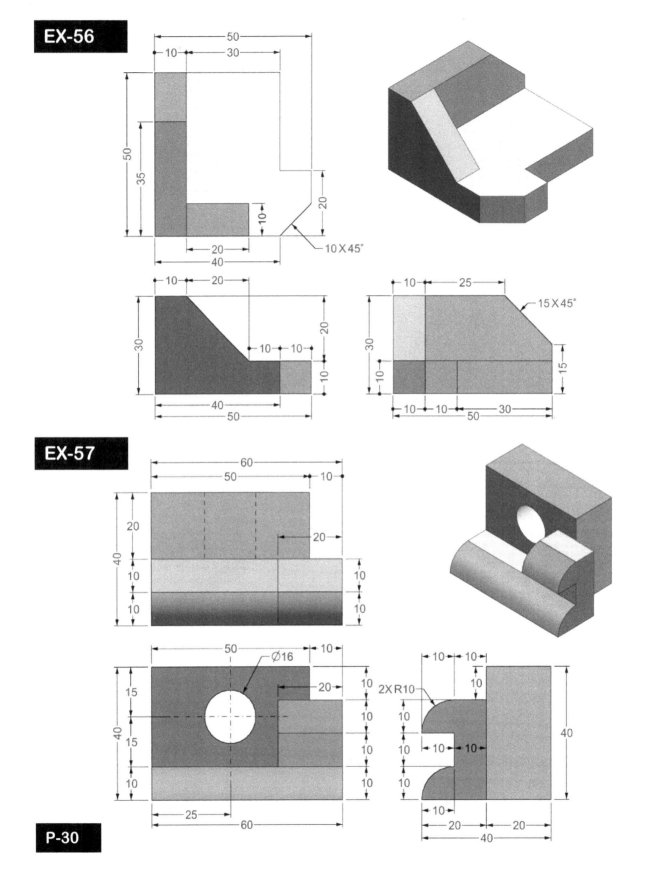

EX-56

50
10 30
50
35
20
10
20
40
10 X 45°

10 20
30
20
10 10
10
40
50

10 25
15 X 45°
30
15
10
10 10 50 30

EX-57

60
50 10
20
40 20
10 10
10 10

50 10
Ø16
20 10
15 10
40 10
15 10
10 10
25
60

10 10
2X R10 10
10
10 10
10 40
10
10
20 20
40

P-30

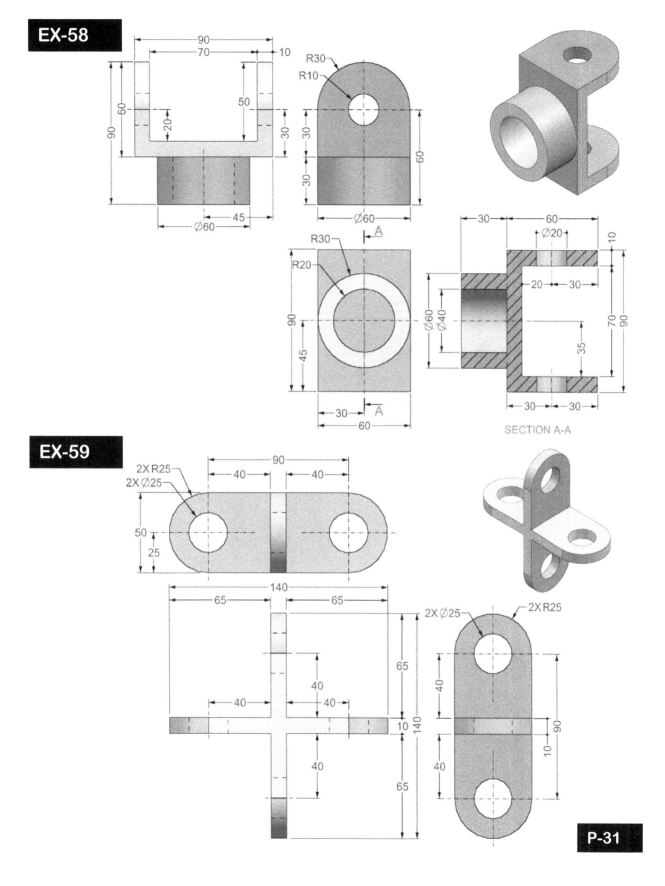

EX-58

EX-59

SECTION A-A

2X R25
2X Ø25

2X Ø25
2X R25

P-31

Ø50
22.5 — 2X Ø10
15
25
43.9
10
60
50
45
15
25
95

Ø50
Ø40
R4 — R10
R10
10
40
155
130
10
45 — 45
80
140
R10
R10
55
30
40
10 — 22.5
10 — 22.5
100

60
85.4
100
155
34.6
10 — 25
40
60

Ø120
20
R3
50
Ø50
R2
10 10 10
Ø50
Ø70

14 14
PCD Ø90
R60
Ø70
Ø30
Ø50
6X Ø10
66
132
14
14
A — A
66
66 — 66
132

132
Ø70
Ø50
Ø30
Ø10
10 10 10
R2
Ø50
Ø80
50
100
R3
Ø10
45 — 45
90
Ø120
20

SECTION A-A

Ø120
PCD Ø90
6X Ø10
ON PCD 90
Ø30
66
14
14
132
66
14 14
66 — 66
132

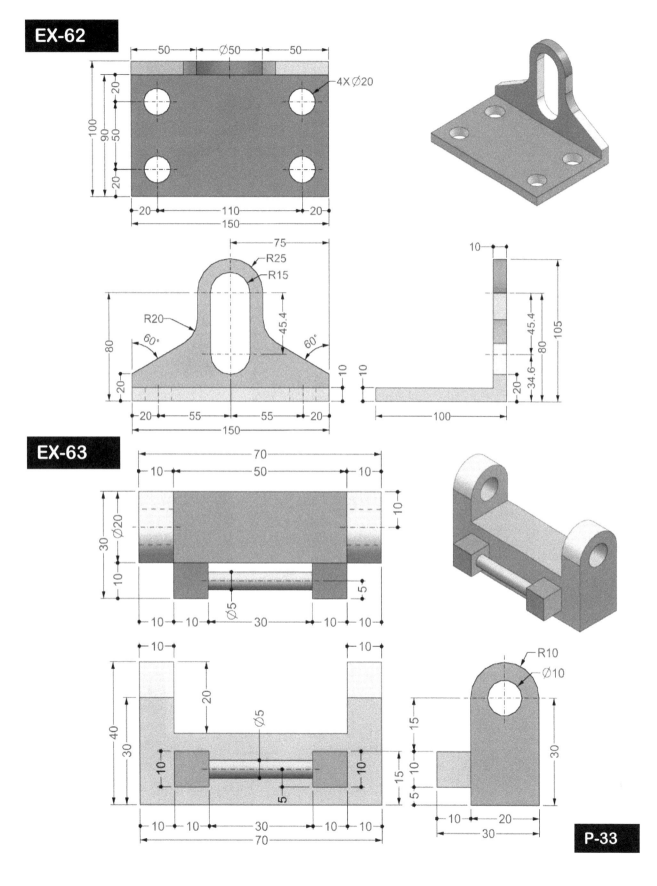

EX-62

EX-63

P-33

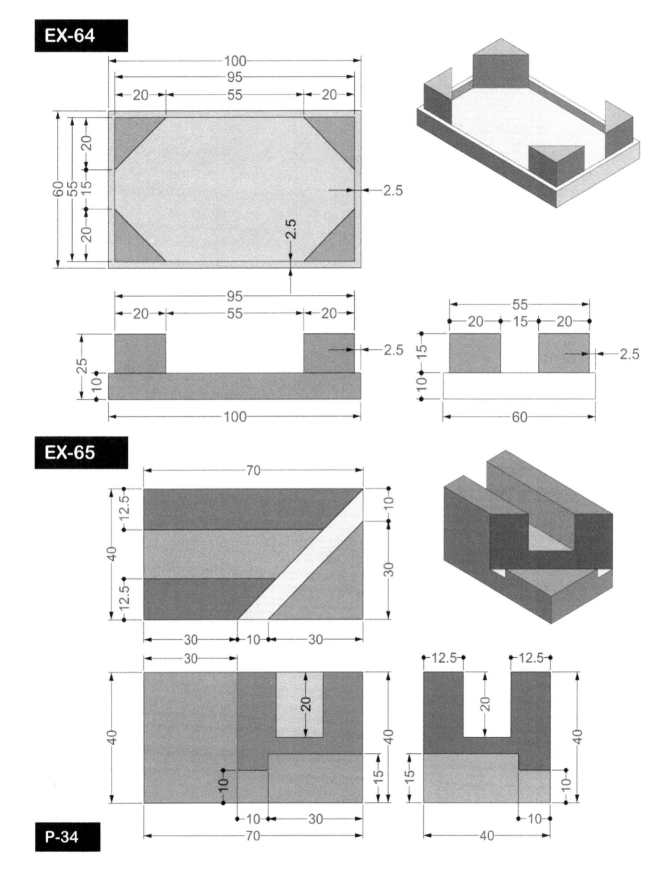

EX-64

EX-65

P-34

EX-66

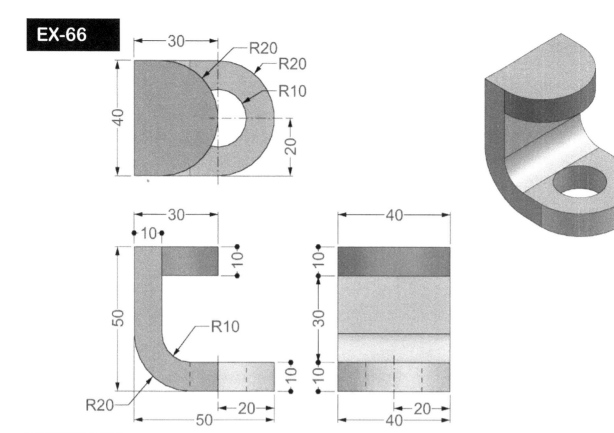

EX-67

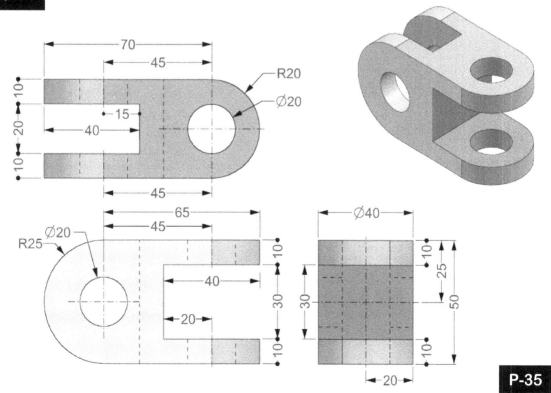

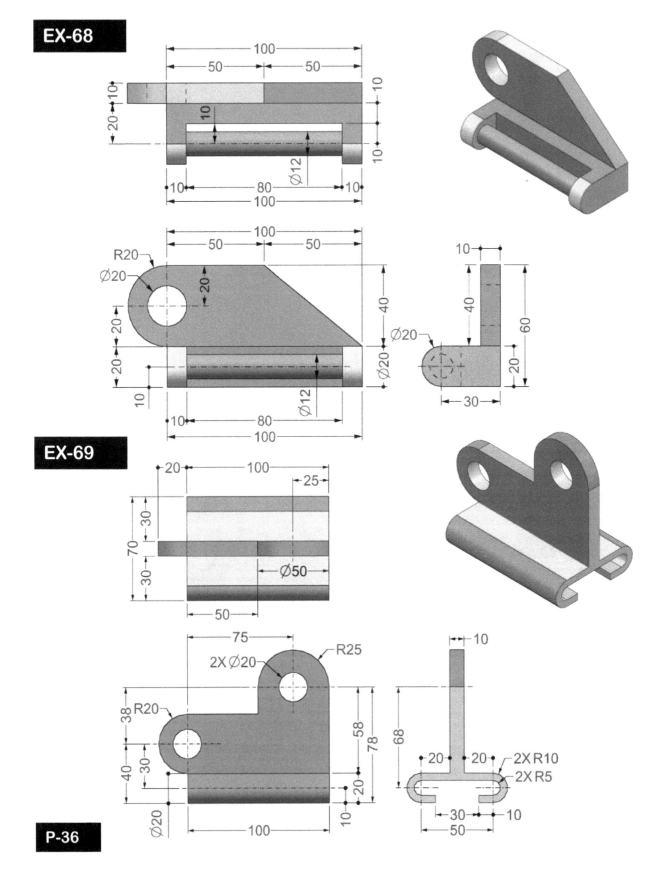

EX-68

EX-69

P-36

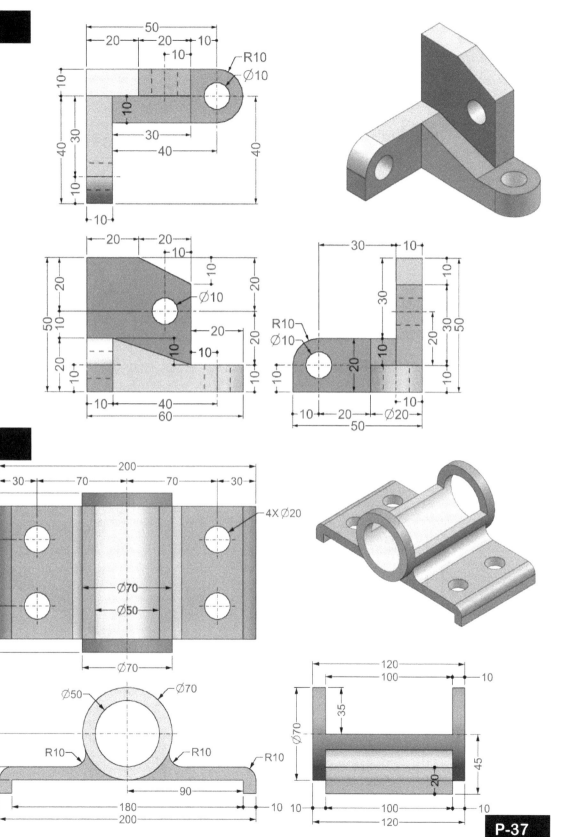

EX-70

EX-71

P-37

EX-72

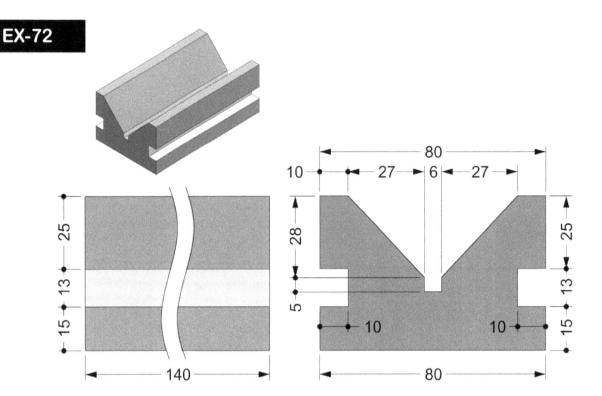

EX-73

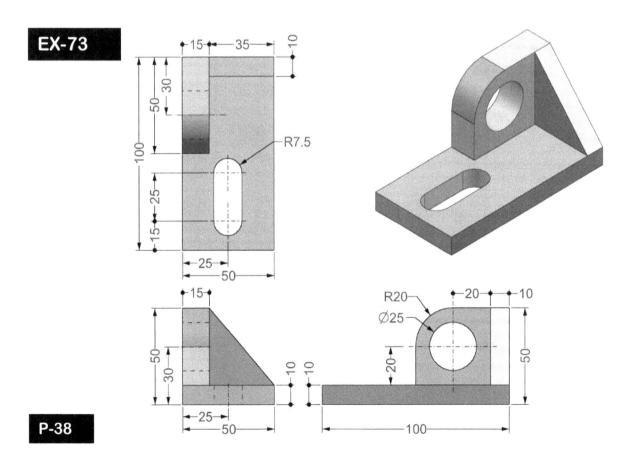

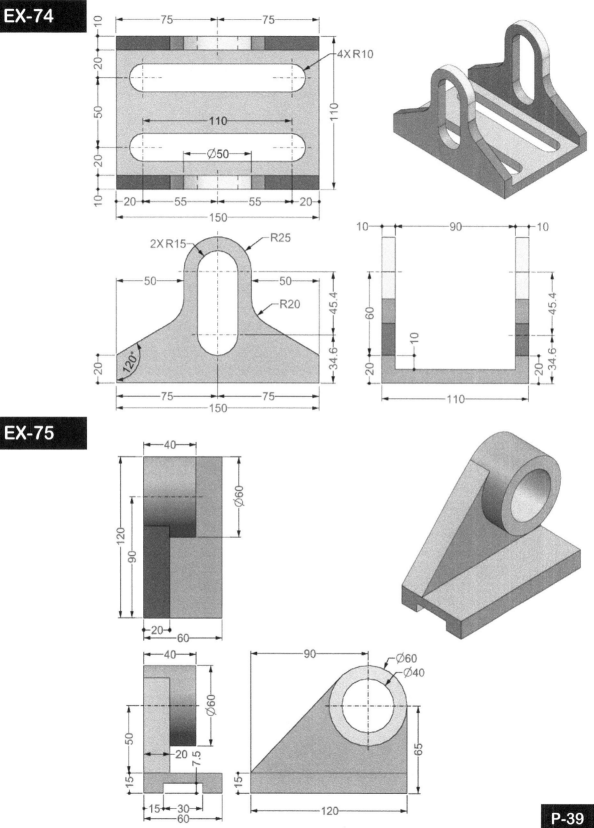

EX-74

75 75
10
20
50
20
10
4X R10
110
110
20 55 55 20
150
⌀50

2X R15 R25
50 50
R20
45.4
34.6
120°
20
75 75
150

10 90 10
60
10
45.4
20 34.6
20
110

EX-75

40
⌀60
120
90
20
60

40
⌀60
50
20 7.5
15
15 30
60

90
⌀60
⌀40
65
15
120

P-39

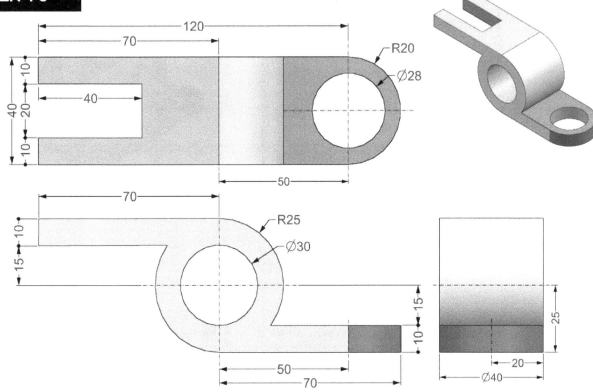

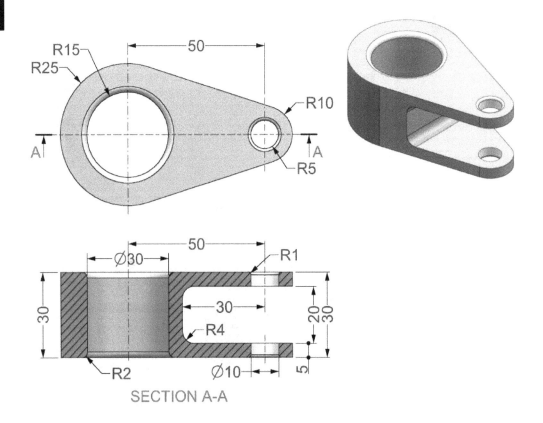

SECTION A-A

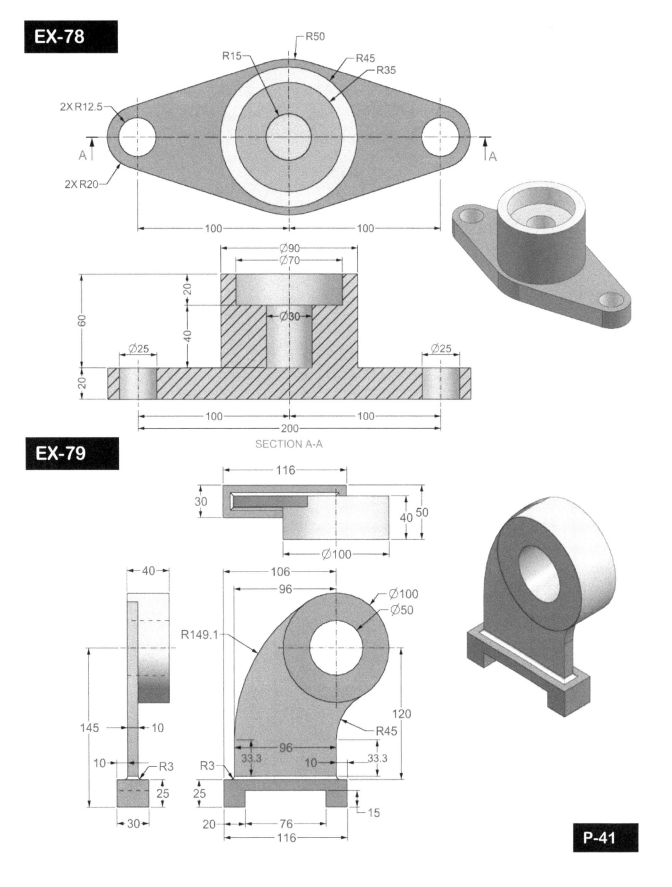

EX-78

R50
R15
R45
R35
2X R12.5
A
2X R20
A
100
100

Ø90
Ø70
20
Ø30
60
40
Ø25
Ø25
20
100
100
200
SECTION A-A

EX-79

116
30
40 50
Ø100

40
106
96
Ø100
Ø50
R149.1
R45
145
10
120
10
R3
96
33.3
10
33.3
R3
25
25
30
15
20
76
116

P-41

4 HOLES, ∅8.6
ON DIA 54 PCD

6 HOLES, ∅10
ON DIA 32 PCD

∅70

∅16

A

A

∅54

∅32

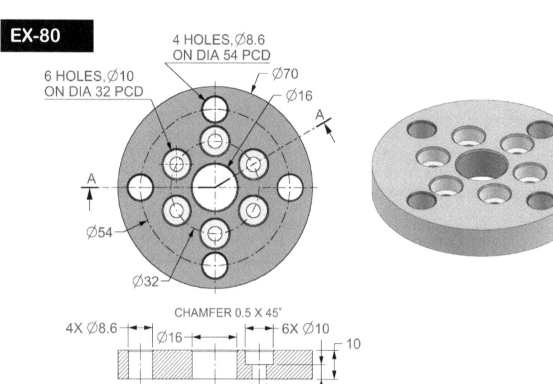

CHAMFER 0.5 X 45°

4X ∅8.6

∅16

6X ∅10

10

5

5

SECTION A-A
(SCALE 1:1)

10

207.2

171.6

17.8

6X ∅8.4

87.2

4X R19.4

19.2

9.6

106

254

254

233.6

190.4

109.8

56.4

36.6

38 28

10

2X R11.6

60

10

103.6

147.2

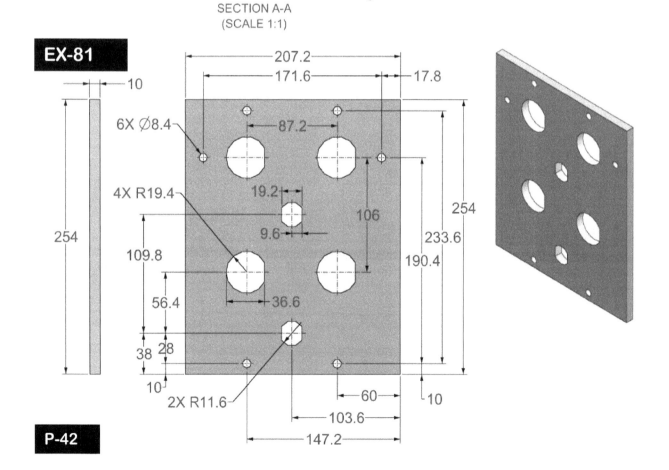

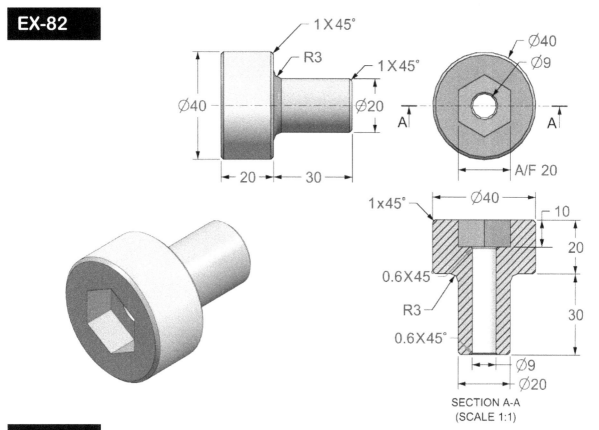

1 X 45°
R3
1 X 45°
∅40
∅20
20
30

∅40
∅9
A
A
A/F 20

1x45°
∅40
10
20
0.6X45°
R3
30
0.6X45°
∅9
∅20

SECTION A-A
(SCALE 1:1)

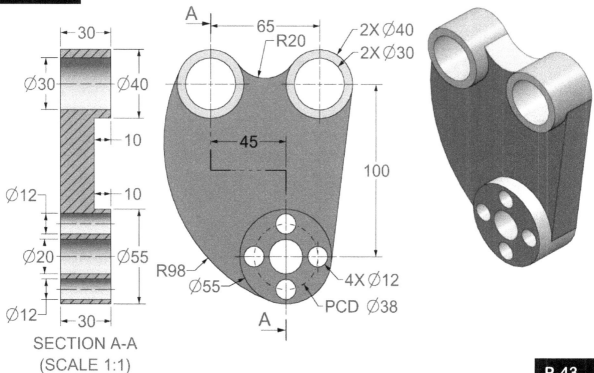

30
∅30
∅40
10
10
∅12
∅20
∅55
∅12
30

SECTION A-A
(SCALE 1:1)

A
65
R20
2X ∅40
2X ∅30
45
100
R98
∅55
4X ∅12
PCD ∅38
A

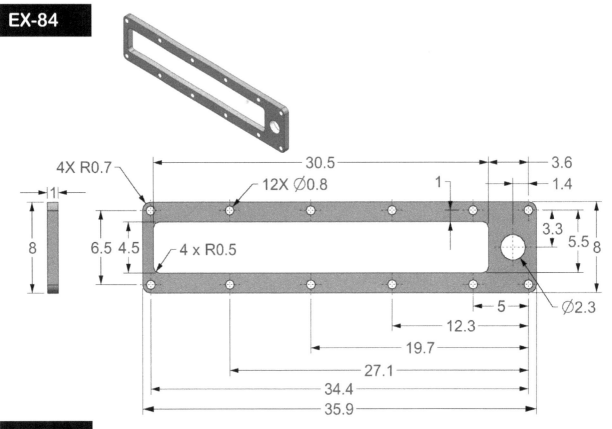

4X R0.7
12X Ø0.8
4 x R0.5
30.5
3.6
1.4
1
3.3
5.5
8
Ø2.3
5
12.3
19.7
27.1
34.4
35.9
6.5 4.5
8
1

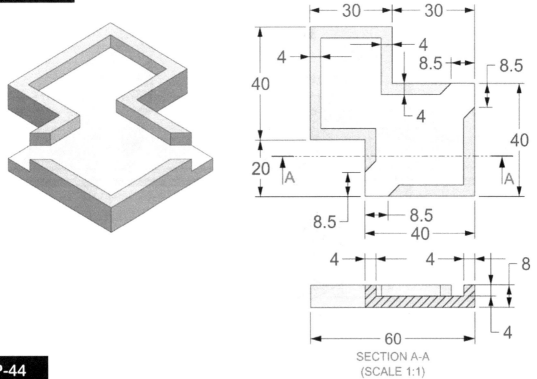

30
30
4
4
8.5
8.5
40
4
40
20
A
A
8.5
8.5
40
8.5
4
4
8
60
4
SECTION A-A
(SCALE 1:1)

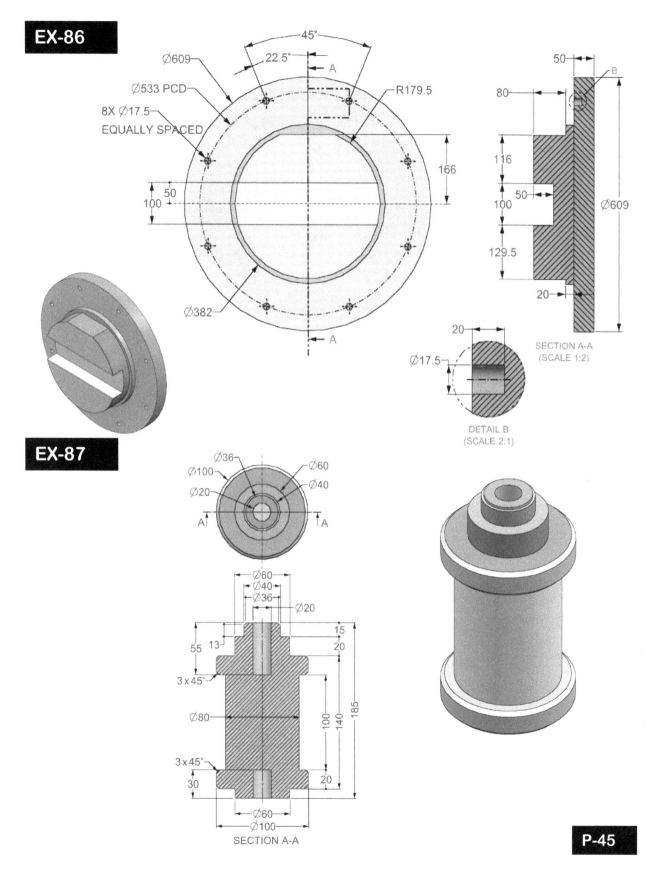

EX-86

Ø609
Ø533 PCD
8X Ø17.5
EQUALLY SPACED
45°
22.5°
A
R179.5
Ø382
166
50
100
A

50
80
B
116
50
100
129.5
20
Ø609
SECTION A-A
(SCALE 1:2)

20
Ø17.5
DETAIL B
(SCALE 2:1)

EX-87

Ø36
Ø100
Ø60
Ø40
Ø20
A
A

Ø60
Ø40
Ø36
Ø20
55
13
15
20
3 x 45°
Ø80
100
140
185
3 x 45°
30
20
Ø60
Ø100
SECTION A-A

P-45

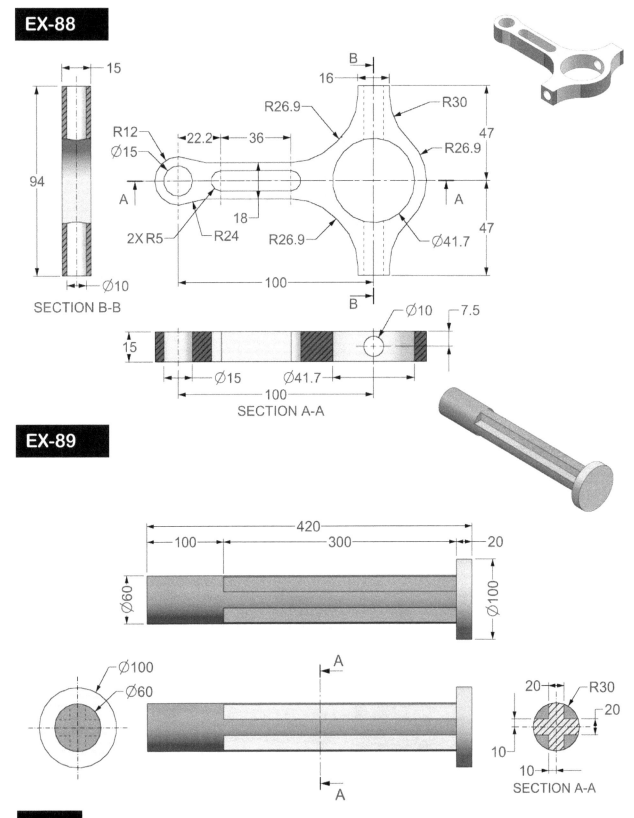

EX-88

94

15

SECTION B-B

Ø10

R12
Ø15
22.2
36
R26.9
16
B
R30
47
R26.9
47
R26.9
Ø41.7
A
A
2X R5
R24
18
100
B

Ø10
7.5
15
Ø15
Ø41.7
100
SECTION A-A

EX-89

420
100
300
20
Ø60
Ø100

Ø100
Ø60
A
A

20
R30
20
10
10
SECTION A-A

P-46

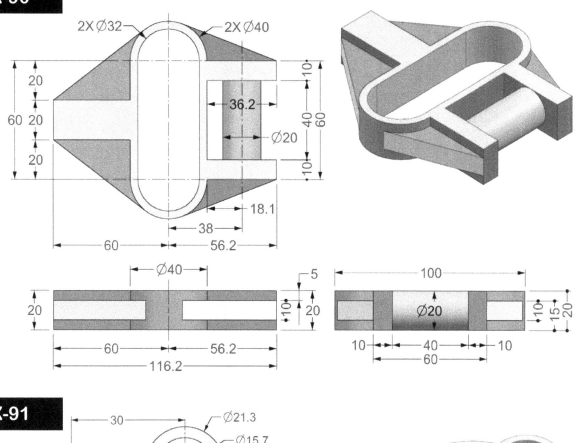

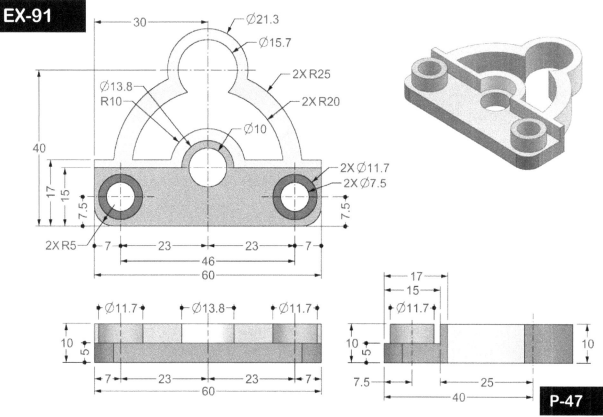

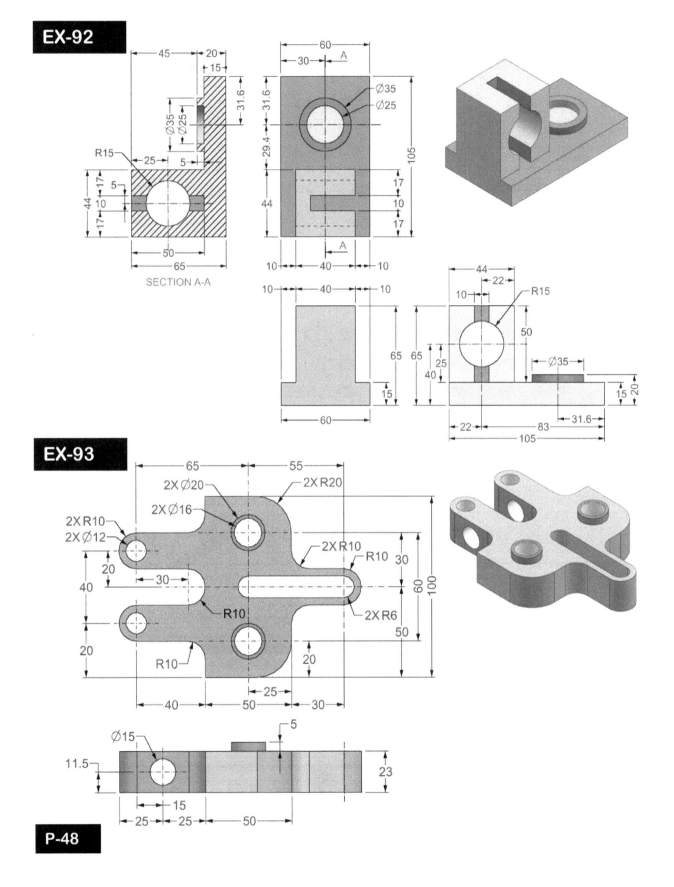

EX-92

SECTION A-A

EX-93

P-48

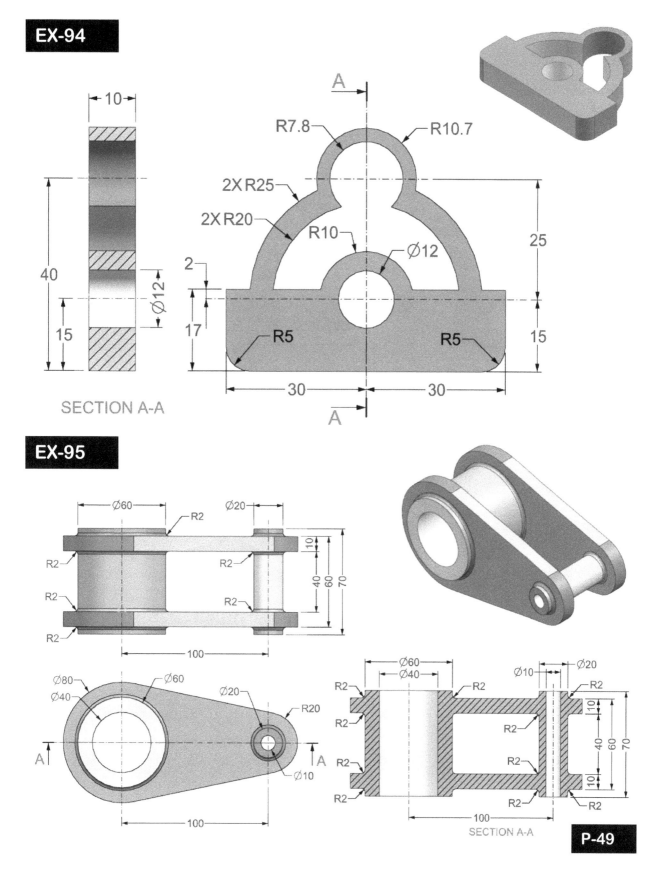

EX-94

10

40

15

Ø12

SECTION A-A

A

R7.8   R10.7

2X R25

2X R20   R10   Ø12

2   25

17

15

R5   R5

30   30

A

EX-95

Ø60   R2   Ø20

R2   R2

R2   R2

10

40

60

70

100

Ø80   Ø60   Ø20

Ø40   R20

A   A

Ø10

100

Ø60   Ø10   Ø20

Ø40

R2   R2   R2

R2   R2

10

40

60

70

R2   R2

R2   R2

R2   R2

100

SECTION A-A

P-49

EX-96

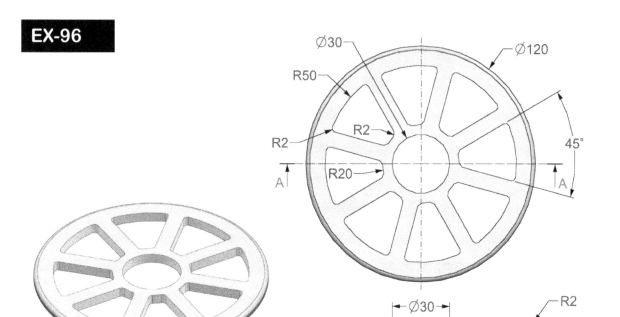

Ø30
Ø120
R50
R2
R2
R2
R20
45°
A
A

Ø30
Ø120
R2
R2
SECTION A-A

EX-97

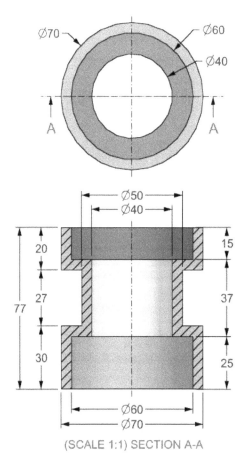
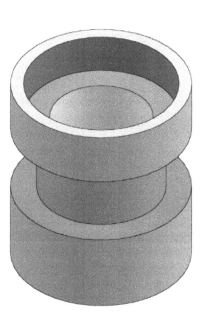

Ø70
Ø60
Ø40
A
A

Ø50
Ø40
20
15
27
37
77
30
25
Ø60
Ø70
(SCALE 1:1) SECTION A-A

P-50

EX-98

100
20 — 60 — 20
5 X 45°
15
15
30
4X Ø16
170
140
50 15 15
70
30
15
15

100
15 — 70 — 15
70
60
100

60 — 50 — 60
30 — 30 — 30 — 30
70
60
60
10
36.2 — 30 — 37.6 — 30 — 36.2
10

EX-99

ON PCD Ø41
Ø2
Ø36
Ø46
Ø16
Ø46
Ø36
Ø16
Ø36
A
A
5
5 5 — 20 — 5 5
40
SECTION A-A

Ø46
Ø36
Ø2
5 5
20
40
5 5
5
Ø36
Ø46

P-51

EX-100

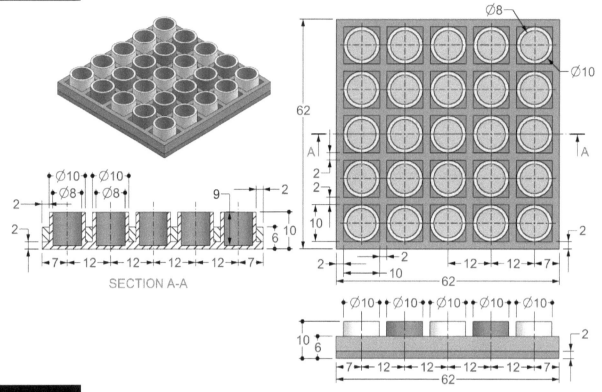

SECTION A-A

EX-101

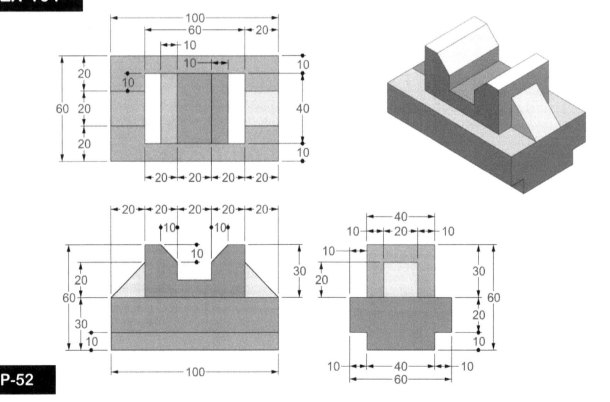

P-52

EX-102

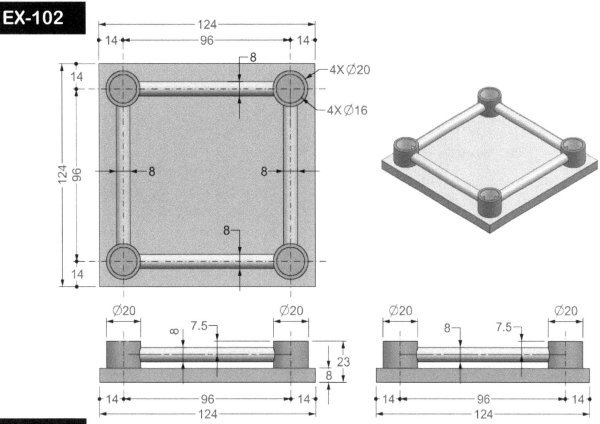

EX-103

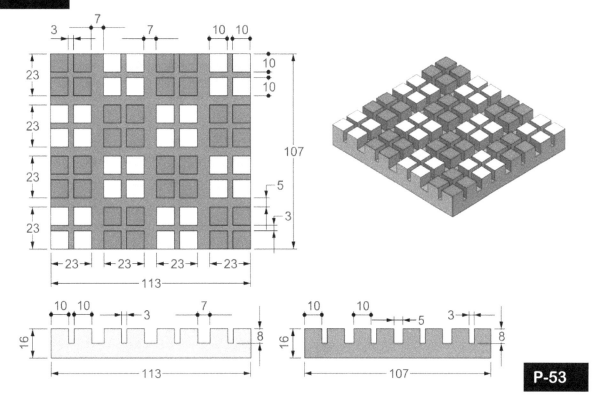

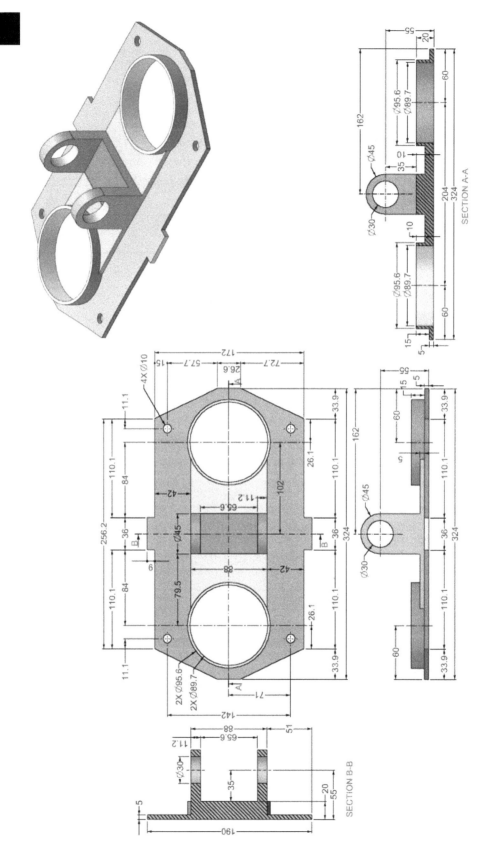

SECTION A-A

SECTION B-B

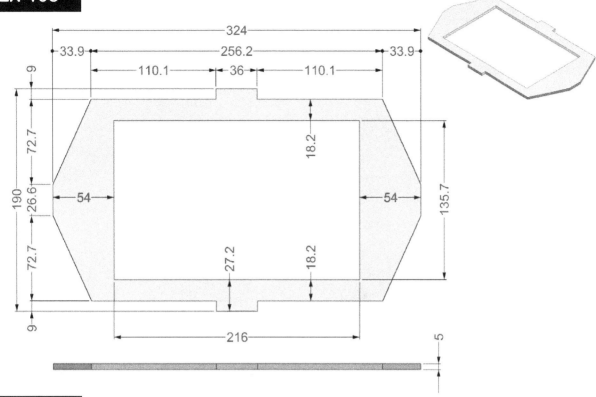

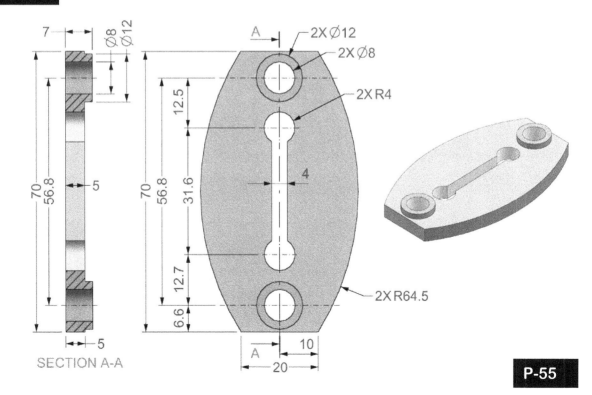

SECTION A-A

EX-107

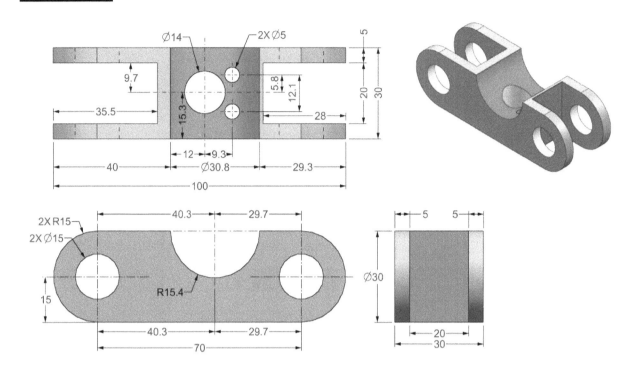

EX-108

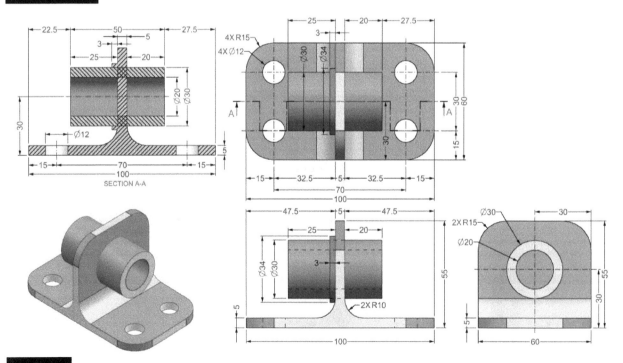

SECTION A-A

P-56

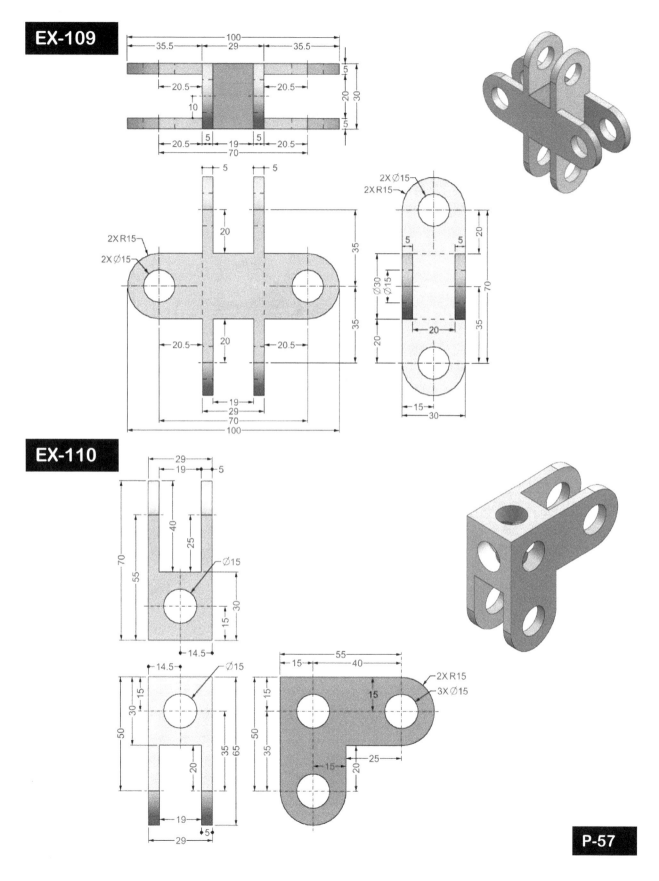

EX-109

EX-110

EX-111

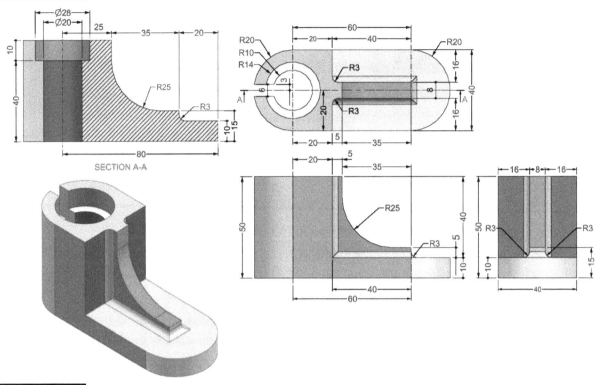

SECTION A-A

EX-112

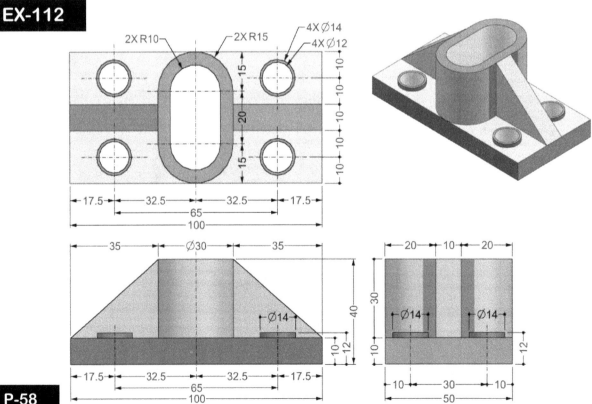

P-58

EX-113

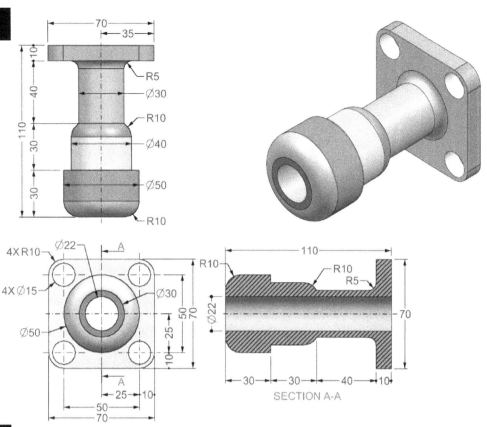

4X R10
Ø22
4X Ø15
Ø30
Ø50
50
70
25
10
25 10
50
70

SECTION A-A

R10
R10
R5
Ø22
70
30 30 40 10

EX-114

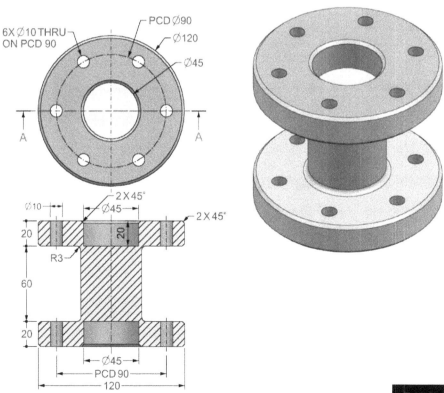

6X Ø10 THRU
ON PCD 90
PCD Ø90
Ø120
Ø45

2 X 45°
Ø10
Ø45
2 X 45°
20
20
R3
60
20
Ø45
PCD 90
120

SECTION A-A

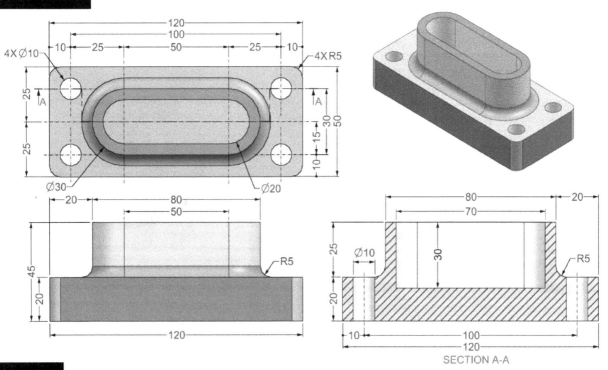

EX-115

Ø120
6X Ø10
6X Ø8
PCD Ø90
Ø68
Ø45

A — A

Ø120
Ø68
R2
Ø10
10
10
20
120
60
20
10
PCD 90

Ø120
PCD 90
Ø68
Ø45
Ø10
2 X 45°
40
20
20
60
R3
Ø8
Ø55
R3
Ø50
20
20
20
Ø45
Ø8

SECTION A-A

EX-116

120
100
10
25
50
25
10
4X Ø10
4X R5
25
A
A
25
30
50
15
10
Ø30
Ø20

20
80
50
45
20
R5
120

80
20
70
25
Ø10
30
R5
10
100
120

SECTION A-A

P-60

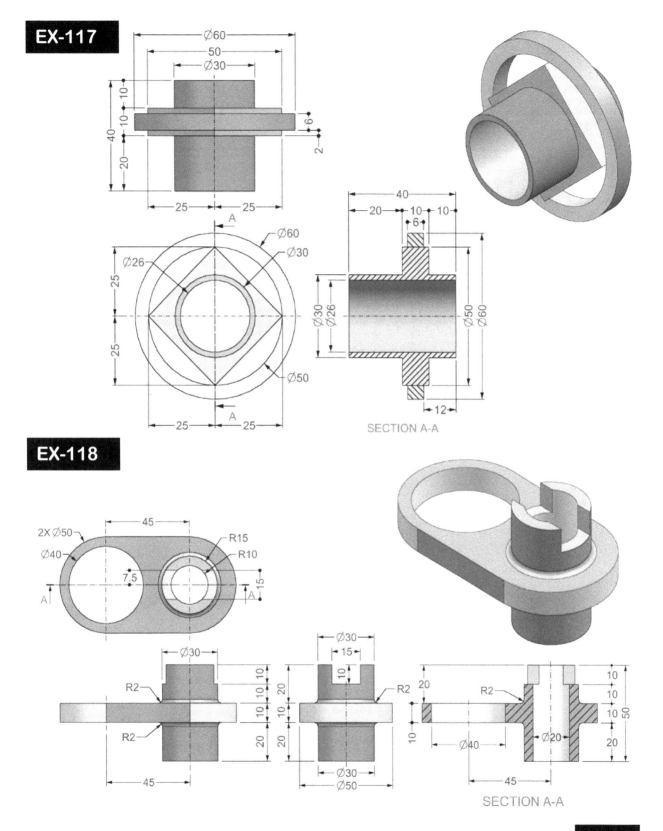

EX-117

Ø60
50
Ø30
10
10
40
20
25
25

A

Ø60
Ø30
Ø26
Ø50
25
25
25
25

A

40
20
10
10
6
Ø30
Ø26
Ø50
Ø60
12

SECTION A-A

EX-118

2X Ø50
Ø40
R15
R10
7.5
15
45
A
A

Ø30
R2
R2
10
10
10
10
20
45

Ø30
15
10
20
10
20
R2
Ø30
Ø50

Ø30
20
R2
Ø40
Ø20
45
10
10
10
50
20
10

SECTION A-A

P-61

EX-119

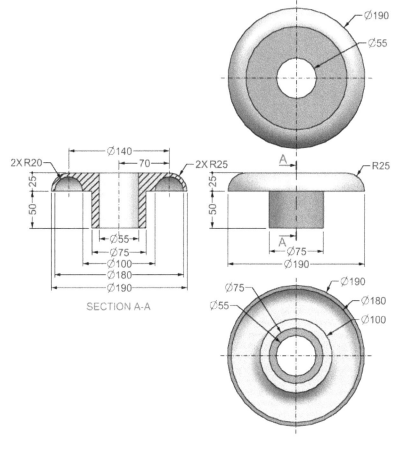

Ø140

70

2X R20

2X R25

25

50

Ø55

Ø75

Ø100

Ø180

Ø190

SECTION A-A

Ø190

Ø55

A

25

50

R25

A

Ø75

Ø190

Ø75

Ø55

Ø190

Ø180

Ø100

EX-120

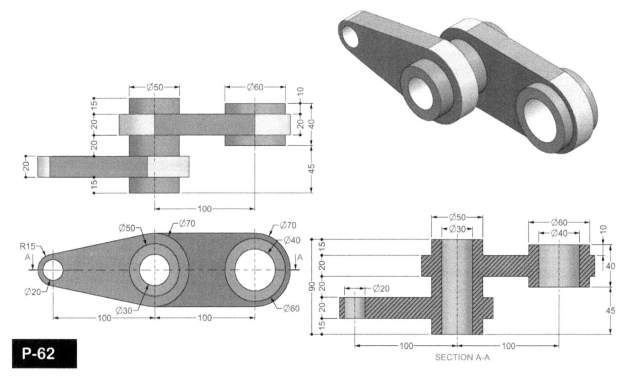

Ø50

Ø60

15

20

20

20

10

20

40

20

15

45

100

R15

A

Ø50

Ø70

Ø70

Ø40

A

Ø20

Ø30

Ø60

100

100

Ø50

Ø30

Ø60

Ø40

15

20

20

20

10

90

Ø20

40

15

20

45

100

100

SECTION A-A

P-62

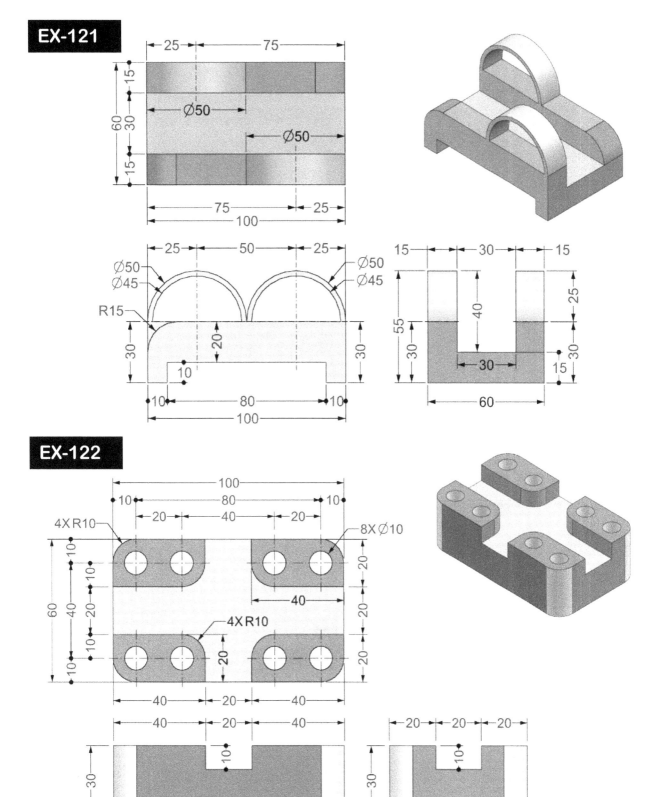

EX-121

EX-122

P-63

EX-123

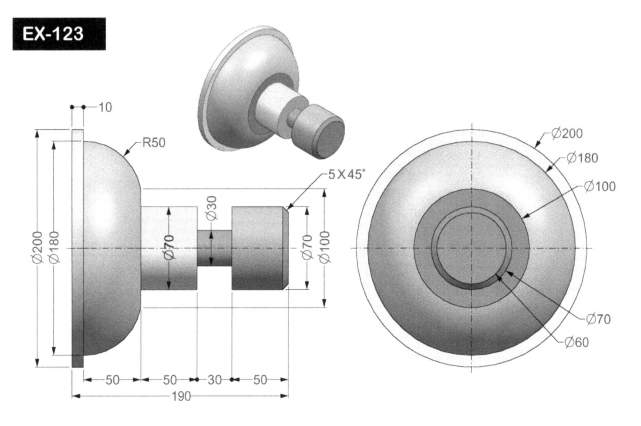

EX-124

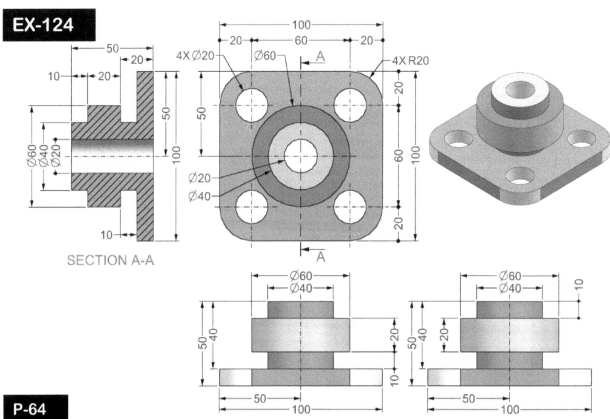

SECTION A-A

P-64

EX-125

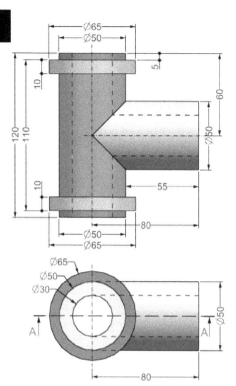

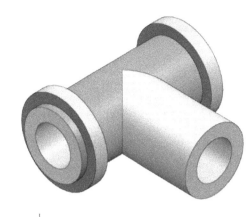

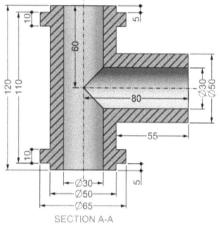

SECTION A-A

EX-126

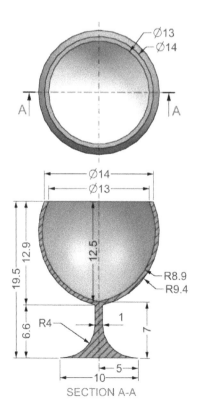

SECTION A-A

P-65

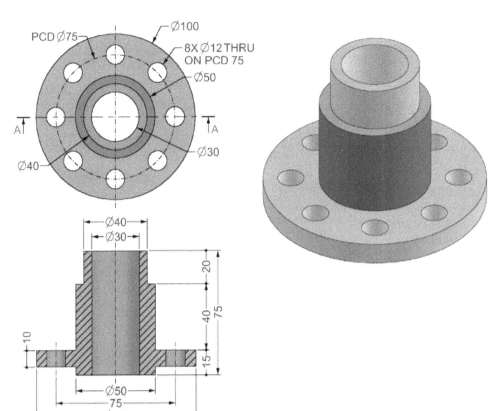

PCD Ø75
Ø100
8X Ø12 THRU
ON PCD 75
Ø50
A
A
Ø30
Ø40

Ø40
Ø30
20
40
75
10
15
Ø50
75
Ø100
SECTION A-A

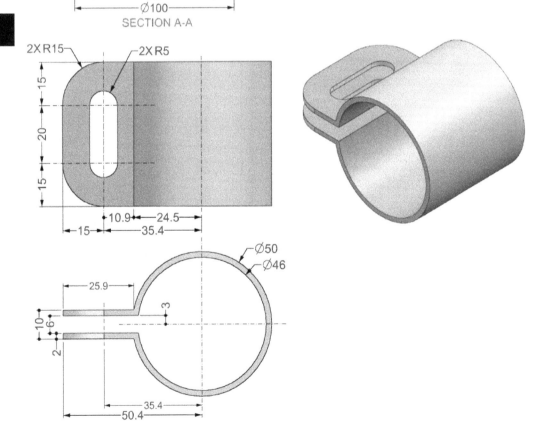

2X R15
2X R5
15
20
15
10.9
24.5
35.4
15

25.9
3
Ø50
Ø46
10
6
2
35.4
50.4

EX-129

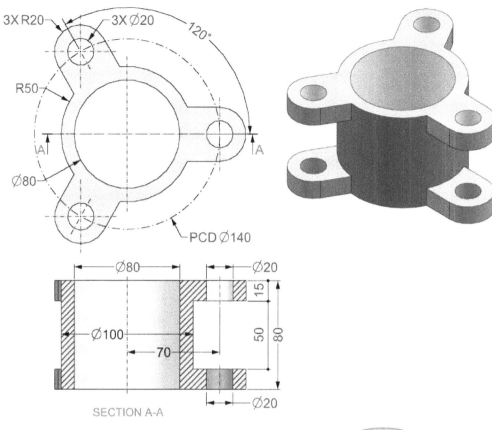

3X R20 3X Ø20 120°

R50

A ⌐ ┐ A

Ø80

PCD Ø140

Ø80 Ø20

15

Ø100

70 50 80

SECTION A-A

Ø20

EX-130

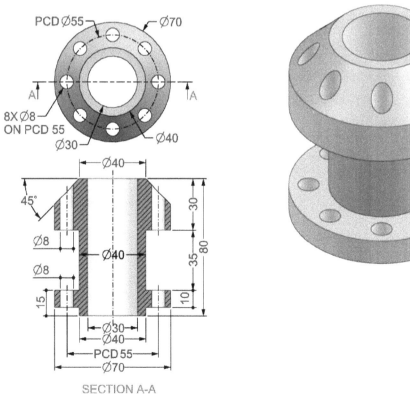

PCD Ø55 Ø70

A ⌐ ┐ A

8X Ø8
ON PCD 55
Ø30 Ø40

Ø40

45°

Ø8

30

Ø40

80

Ø8

35

15

10

Ø30
Ø40
PCD 55
Ø70

SECTION A-A

EX-131

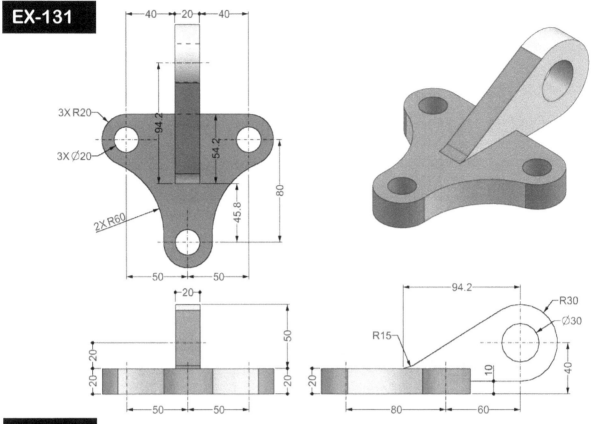

EX-132

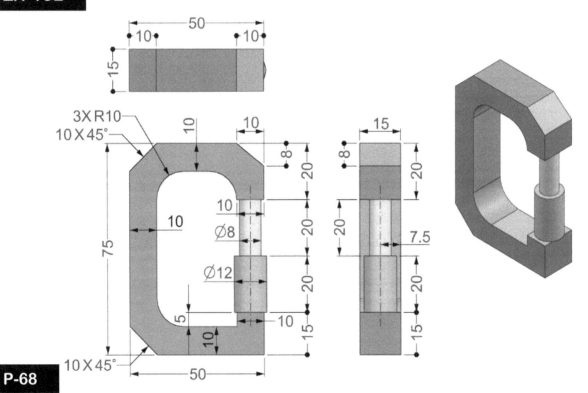

EX-133

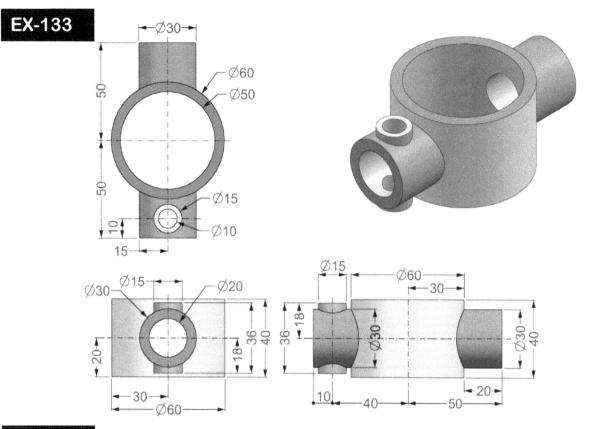

EX-134

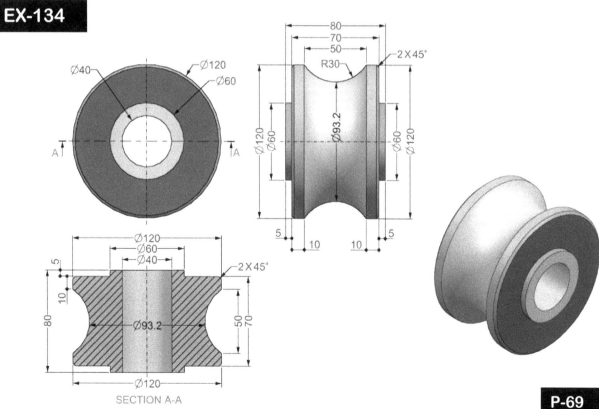

SECTION A-A

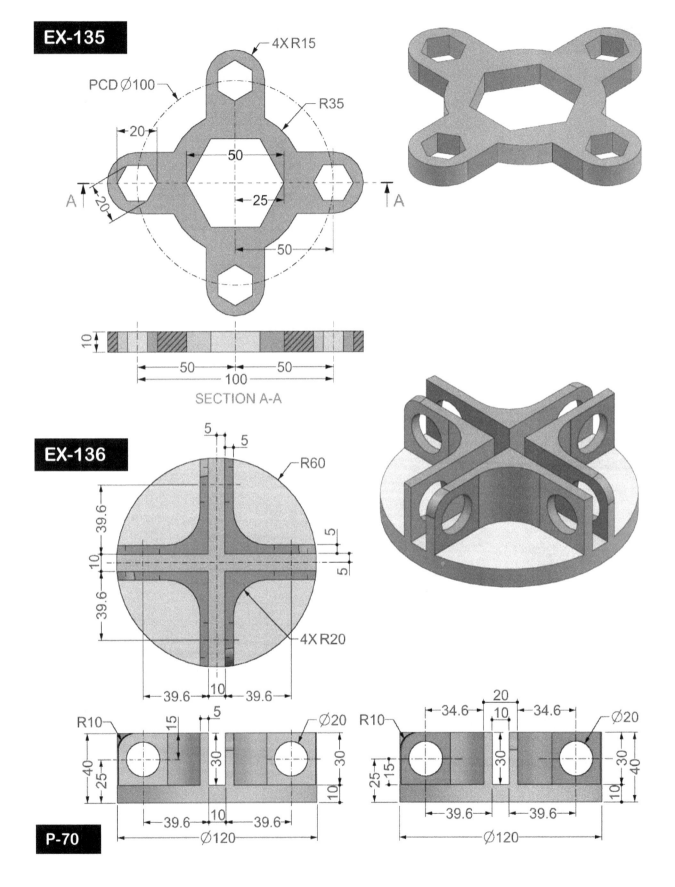

EX-135

PCD Ø100

4X R15

R35

20

50

25

50

A — A

20

SECTION A-A

10

50

50

100

EX-136

5

5

R60

39.6

10

5

5

5

39.6

4X R20

39.6

10

39.6

R10

5

15

30

Ø20

40

25

30

39.6

10

39.6

10

Ø120

R10

20

34.6

10

34.6

Ø20

30

25

15

30

40

39.6

39.6

10

Ø120

P-70

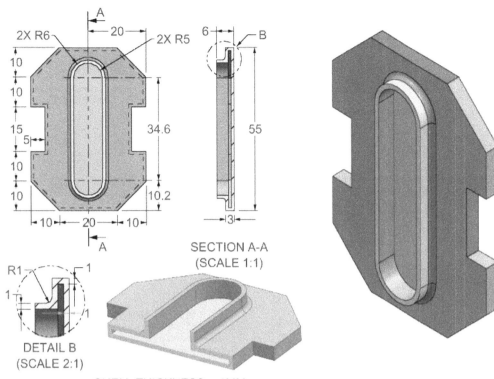

2X R6
2X R5
20
10
10
15
5
10
10
10
20
10
34.6
10.2

6
B
55
3

SECTION A-A
(SCALE 1:1)

R1
1
1
1

DETAIL B
(SCALE 2:1)

SHELL THICKNESS = 1MM
ALL INSIDE WALL THICKNESS

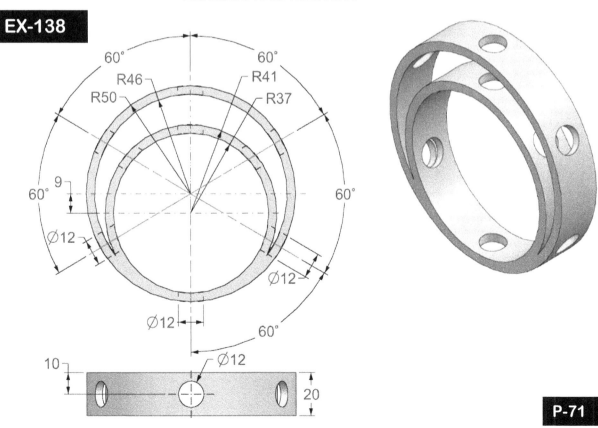

60°
60°
R46
R41
R50
R37
60°
9
60°
Ø12
Ø12
Ø12
60°
Ø12
10
20

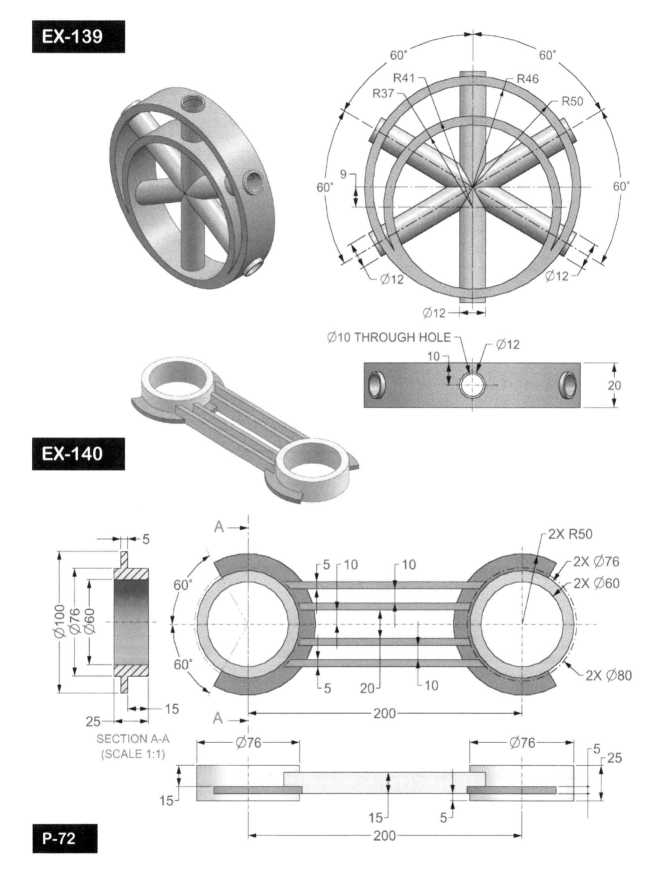

EX-139

R37
R41
R46
R50
60°
60°
60°
60°
9
Ø12
Ø12
Ø12

Ø10 THROUGH HOLE
Ø12
10
20

EX-140

A
5
60°
60°
Ø100
Ø76
Ø60
15
25
SECTION A-A
(SCALE 1:1)

2X R50
2X Ø76
2X Ø60
5 10
10
5
20
10
2X Ø80
200
A

Ø76
Ø76
5
25
15
15
5
200

P-72

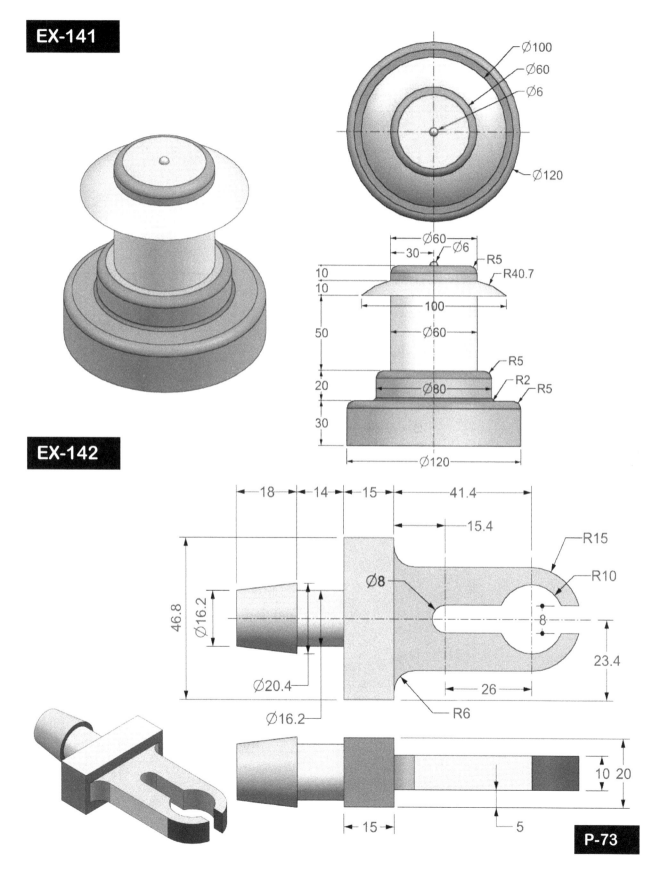

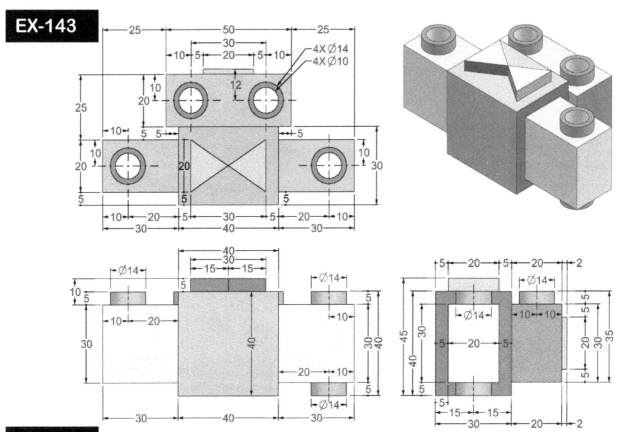

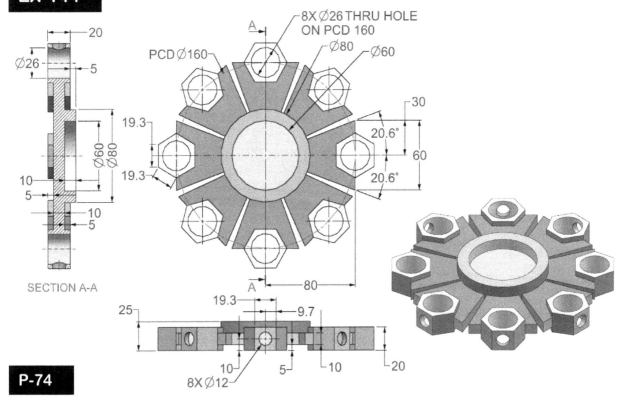

8X Ø26 THRU HOLE
ON PCD 160

PCD Ø160

SECTION A-A

8X Ø12

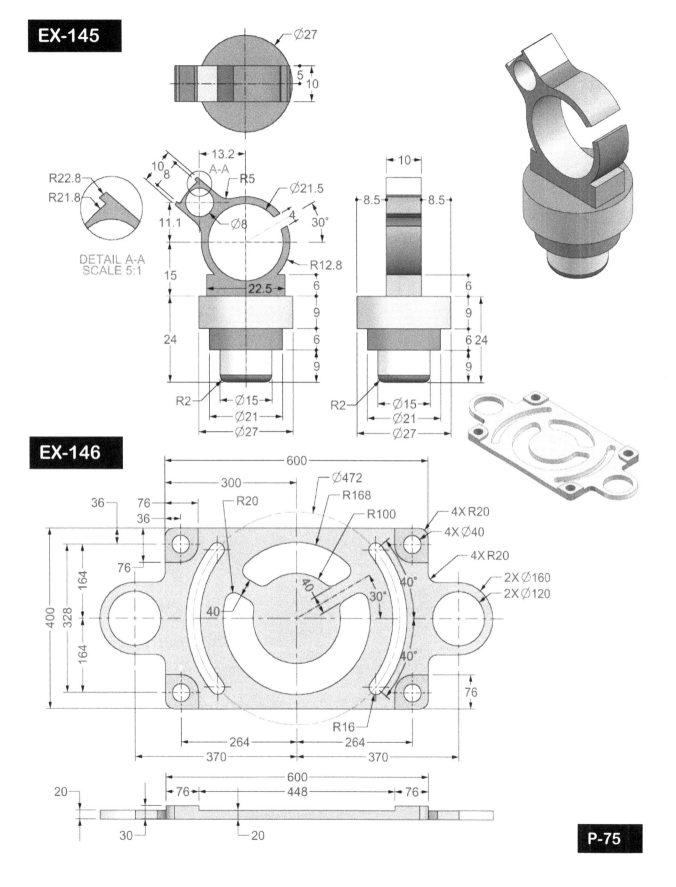

EX-145

Ø27

5
10

13.2

10
8

A-A

R22.8
R21.8

R5

Ø21.5

11.1

Ø8

4

30°

DETAIL A-A
SCALE 5:1

R12.8

15

22.5

24

6
9
6
9

R2

Ø15
Ø21
Ø27

10

8.5   8.5

6
9
6 24
9

R2

Ø15
Ø21
Ø27

EX-146

600

300

Ø472

R168

R20

R100

4X R20
4X Ø40

36
76
36

4X R20

76

2X Ø160
2X Ø120

164

40

40°

400
328

40°
30°

40

40°

164

76

R16

264   264

370   370

600

20

76   448   76

30

20

EX-147

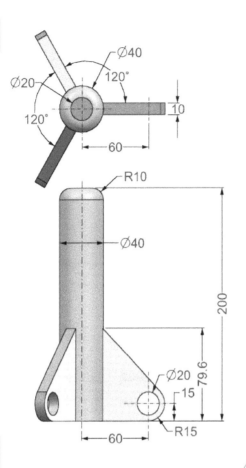

EX-148

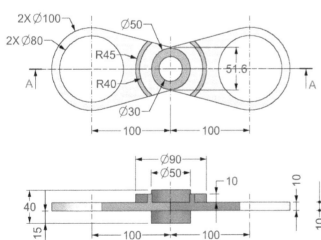

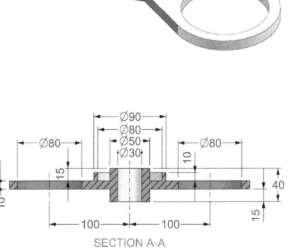

SECTION A-A

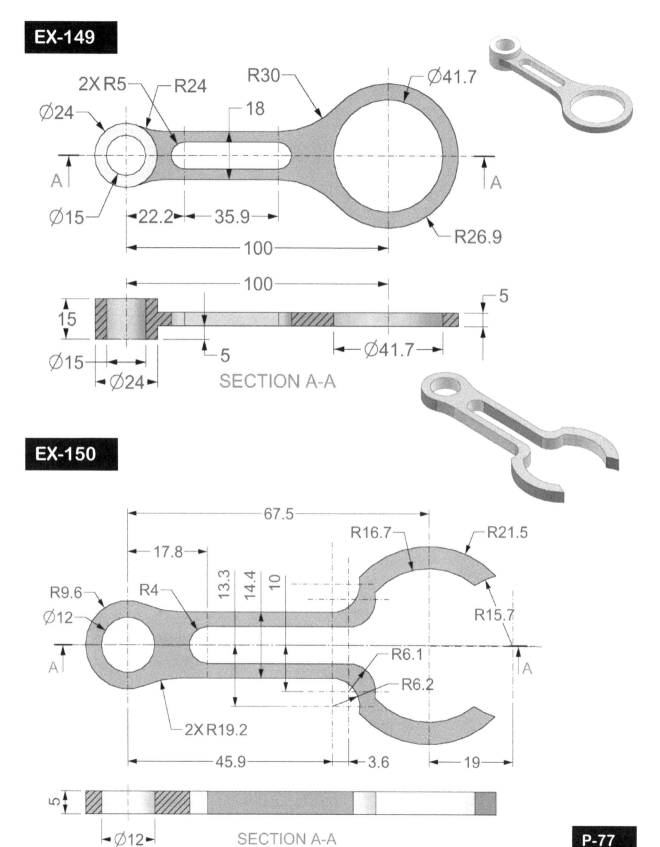

EX-149

2X R5   R24   R30   ⌀41.7

⌀24   18

A

⌀15

22.2   35.9

100

R26.9

100

15   5

⌀15

⌀24   5   ⌀41.7

SECTION A-A

EX-150

67.5

17.8   R16.7   R21.5

R9.6   R4

⌀12   13.3   14.4   10

A   R15.7

R6.1

R6.2

2X R19.2

45.9   3.6   19

5

⌀12   SECTION A-A

Ø8
6,5
10
28
11
R1.5
R1.5
B-B
27
Ø10
SECTION A-A

Ø20
A
R3
35
15°
20
5
A
Ø13.3
Ø16

R8
R6.7
R10
R4
R5

1
45°
DETAIL B-B
SCALE 5:1

Ø20
Ø36
Ø58
Ø52
Ø16

Ø36
Ø20
R8
8
20
2
135°
13.5
Ø16
R11.2
15.8
76
21.6
10.7
13
10
R6
R3
Ø16
SECTION A-A

A
58
3
R3
R2
Ø52
76
R6
A
40

EX-153

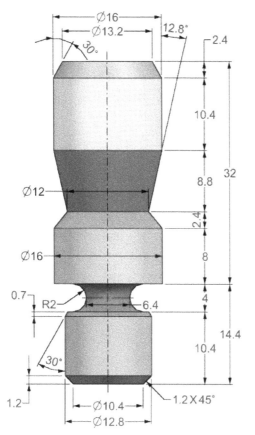

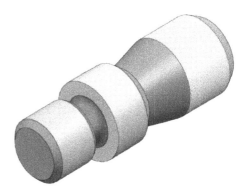

EX-154

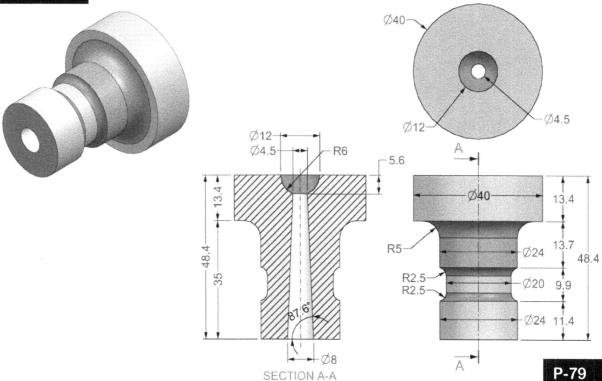

SECTION A-A

P-79

EX-155

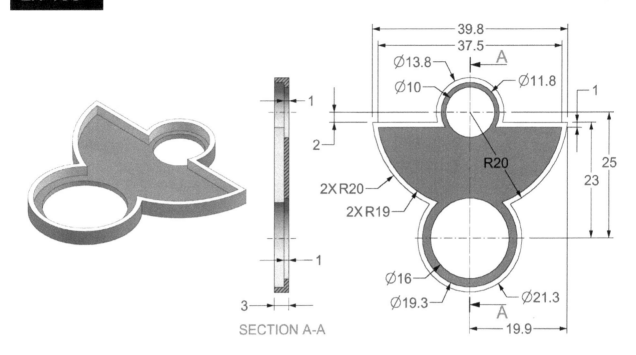

SECTION A-A

EX-156

SECTION A-A

P-80

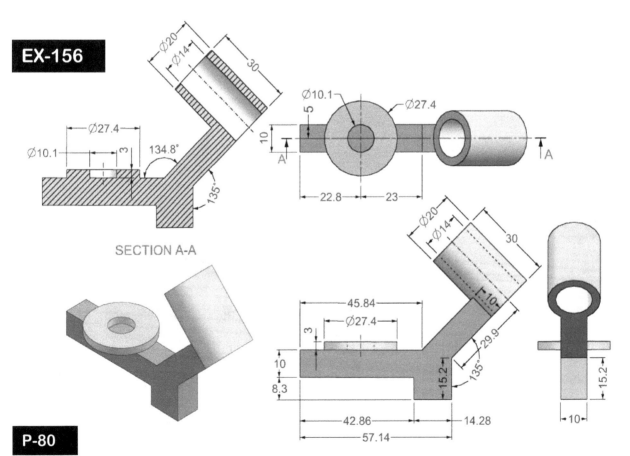

EX-157

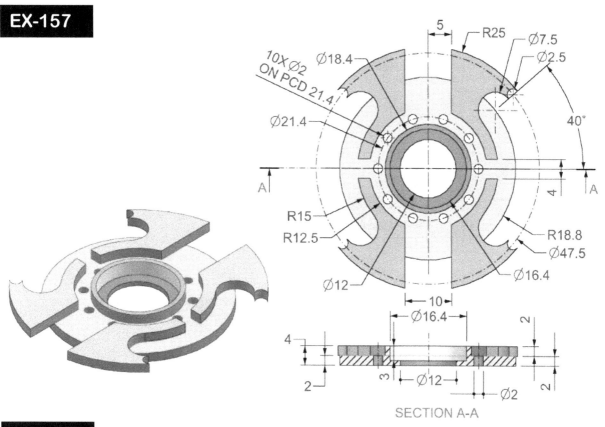

SECTION A-A

EX-158

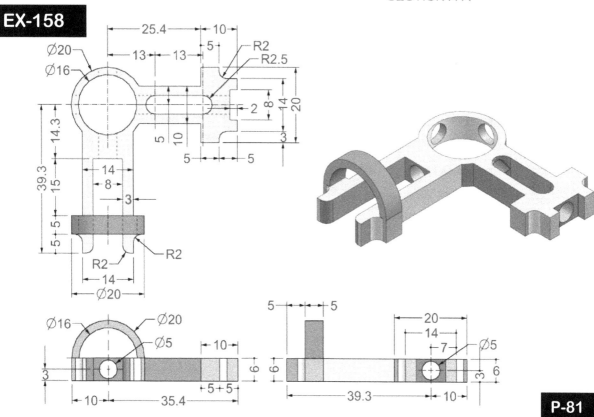

P-81

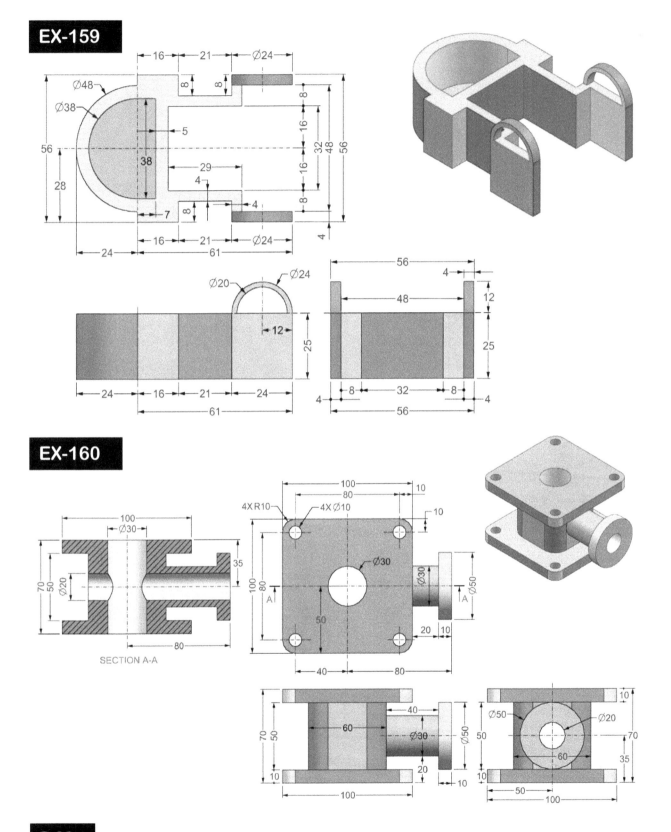

EX-159

EX-160

SECTION A-A

P-82

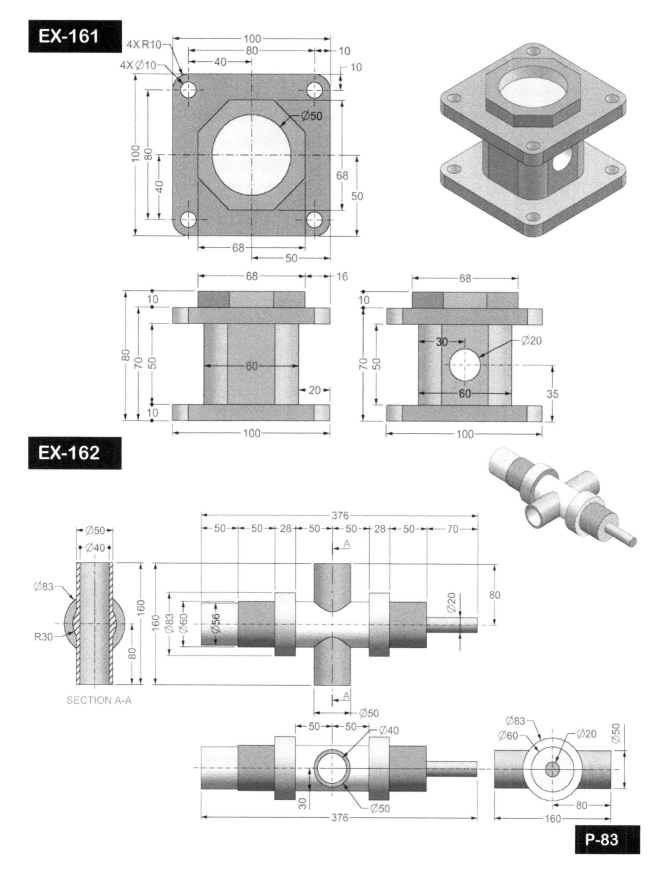

EX-161

4X R10
4X Ø10
100
80
40
10
10
Ø50
100
80
40
68
50
68
50

68
16
10
80
70
50
60
10
20
100

68
10
70
50
30
Ø20
60
35
100

EX-162

376
50 50 28 50 50 28 50 70
A

Ø50
Ø40
Ø83
R30
160
80
SECTION A-A

Ø83
Ø60
Ø56
160
Ø20
80
A

Ø50
50 50 Ø40
Ø50
30
376

Ø83
Ø60
Ø20
Ø50
80
160

P-83

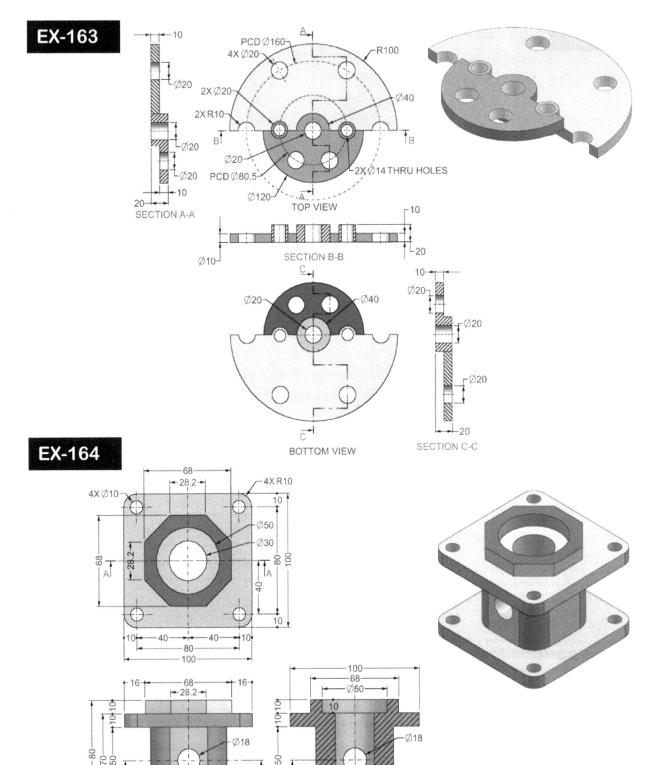

EX-163

SECTION A-A

10
Ø20
Ø20
Ø20
10
20

TOP VIEW

PCD Ø160
4X Ø20
2X Ø20
2X R10
Ø40
Ø20
PCD Ø80.5
2X Ø14 THRU HOLES
Ø120
R100
A
B
B
A

SECTION B-B

10
20
Ø10

BOTTOM VIEW

C
Ø20
Ø40
C

SECTION C-C

10
Ø20
Ø20
Ø20
20

EX-164

68
28.2
4X R10
4X Ø10
10
Ø50
Ø30
68
28.2
A
A
80
100
40
10
10
40
40
10
80
100

16
68
28.2
16
10 10 10
80
70
50
25
10
Ø18
30
60
35
50
100

100
68
Ø50
10 10
10
50
25
10
Ø18
Ø30
50
50
100

SECTION A-A

P-84

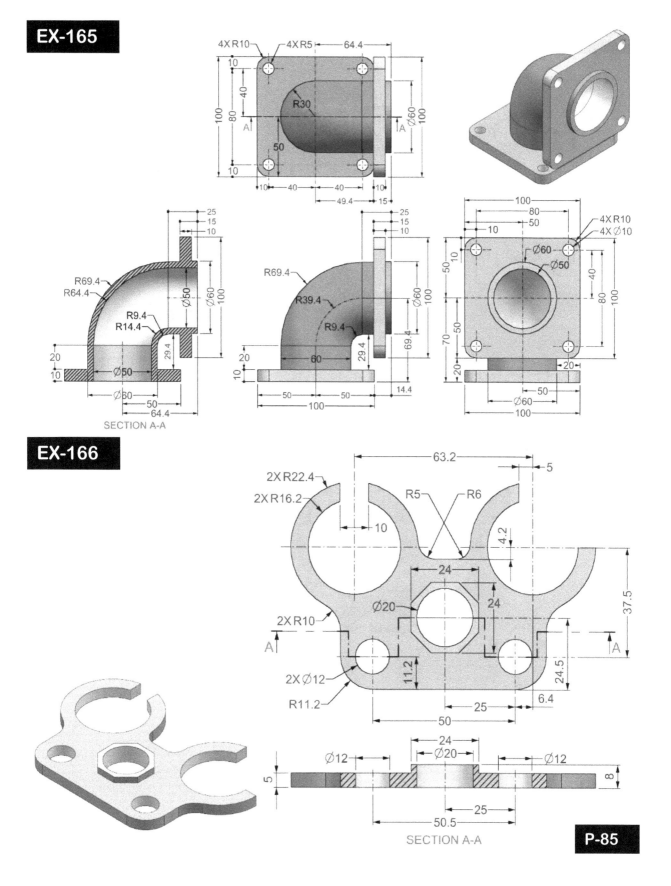

EX-165

R30

4X R10
4X R5
64.4
10
40
80
100
50
10
Ø60
100
A
A
10 40 40 10
49.4 15

R69.4
R64.4
R9.4
R14.4
25
15
10
Ø50
Ø60
100
29.4
20
10
Ø50
Ø60
50
64.4
SECTION A-A

R69.4
R39.4
R9.4
25
15
10
Ø60
100
69.4
29.4
20
10
60
50 50
100
14.4

100
80
50
10
4X R10
4X Ø10
Ø60
Ø50
50
10
40
80
100
70
50
20
20
50
Ø60
100

EX-166

2X R22.4
2X R16.2
63.2
5
R5 R6
10
4.2
24
Ø20
24
37.5
2X R10
A
A
11.2
24.5
2X Ø12
R11.2
25
6.4
50

24
Ø12
Ø20
Ø12
5
8
25
50.5
SECTION A-A

P-85

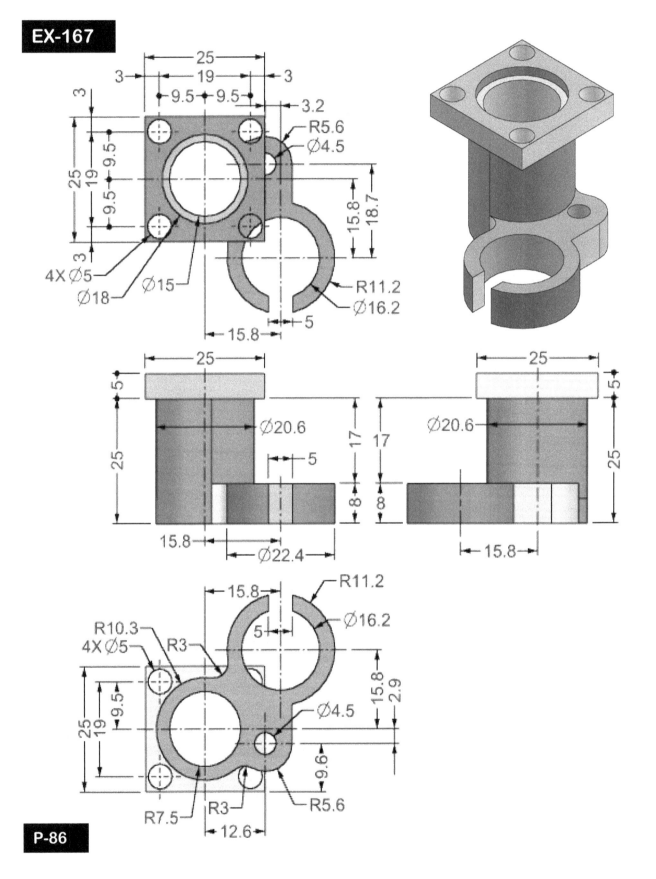

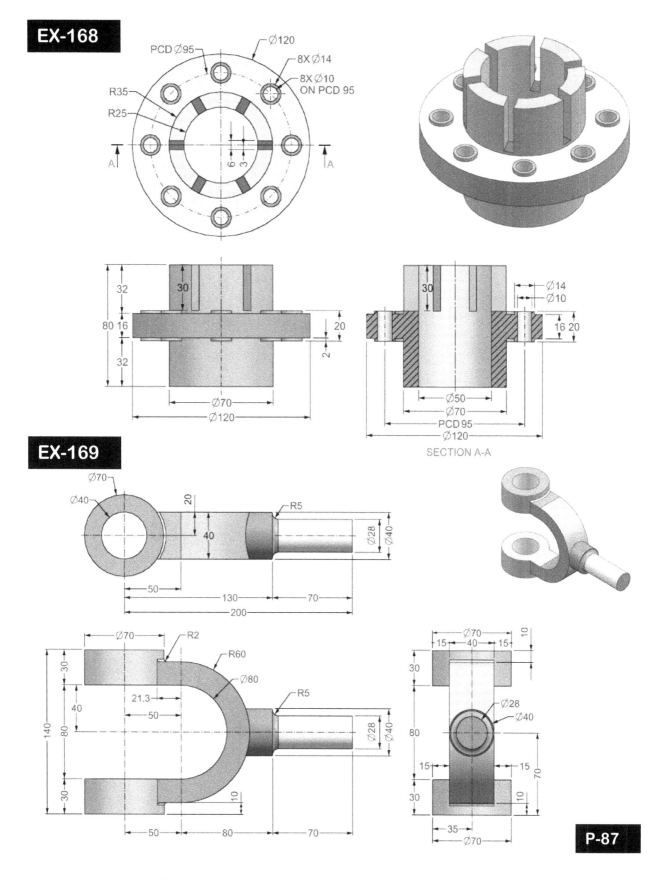

EX-168

PCD Ø95
Ø120
8X Ø14
8X Ø10
ON PCD 95
R35
R25
A
A
6
3

32
30
80 16
32
20
2
Ø70
Ø120

30
Ø14
Ø10
16 20
Ø50
Ø70
PCD 95
Ø120

SECTION A-A

EX-169

Ø70
Ø40
20
40
R5
Ø28
Ø40
50
130
70
200

Ø70
R2
R60
Ø80
R5
30
21.3
50
40
140
80
Ø28
Ø40
30
10
50
80
70

Ø70
15
40
15
10
30
Ø28
Ø40
80
15
15
70
15
30
10
35
Ø70

P-87

EX-170

4X R2
3
2X ∅3
2.75 — 4.75 — ∅15 — 4.75 — 2.75
30
1 — 1 — 1
4
6

R7.5 — R6.5
R2
13
8.5
R2
8.5 — 8.5
15
30

1 — 1
7.5
4
16
1
8.5
6

EX-171

4X ∅23.2
22 — 44 — 184 — 44 — 22
92
R60
138.6
30 — 30
30 — 30
30 — 20
248
168
138.6
124
40
40
80
228
272

40
44 — 20 — 40 — 44
40
264
272
20
35
40

P-88

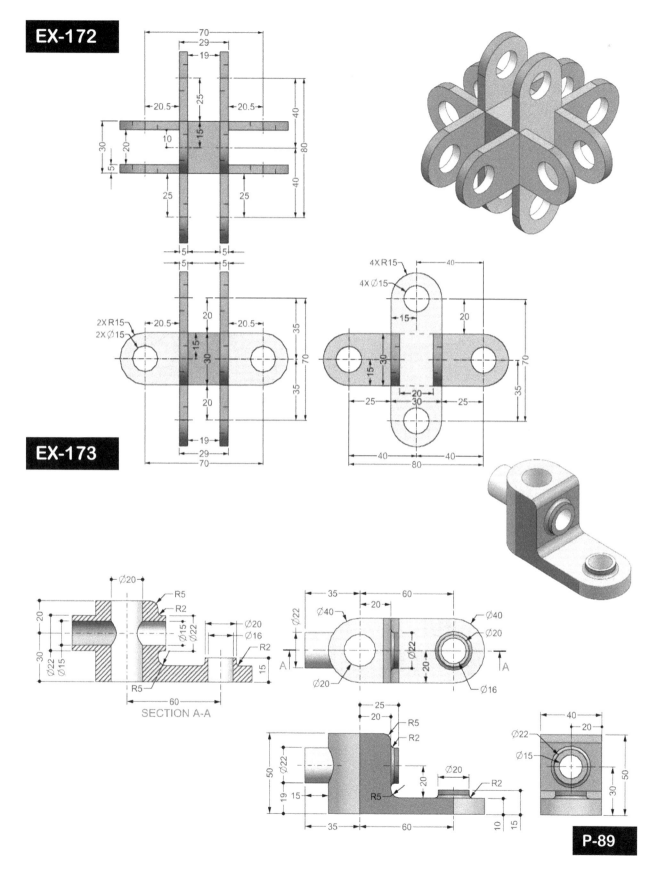

EX-172

EX-173

SECTION A-A

P-89

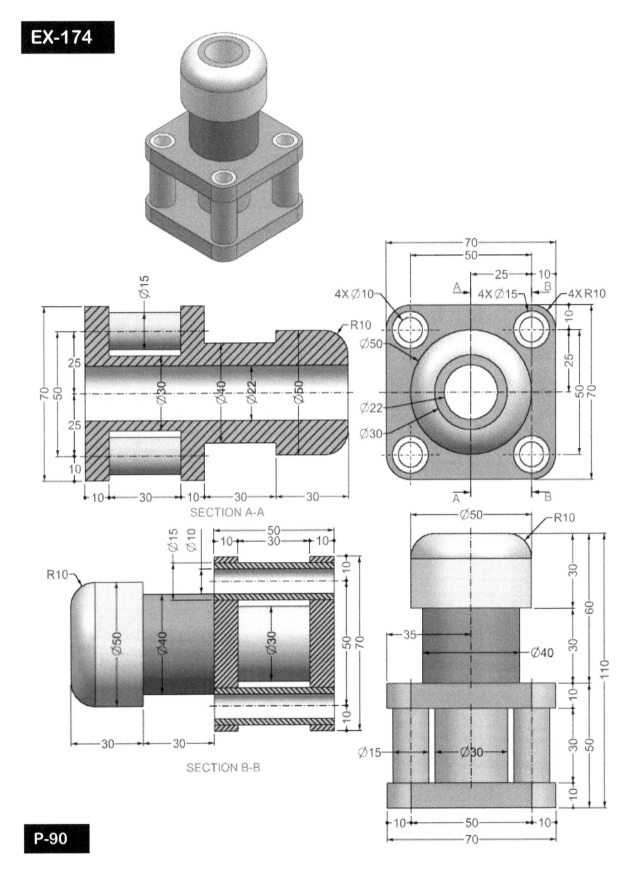

SECTION A-A

SECTION B-B

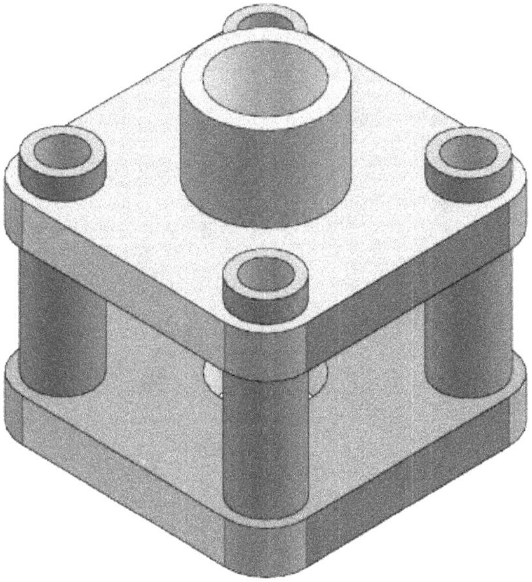

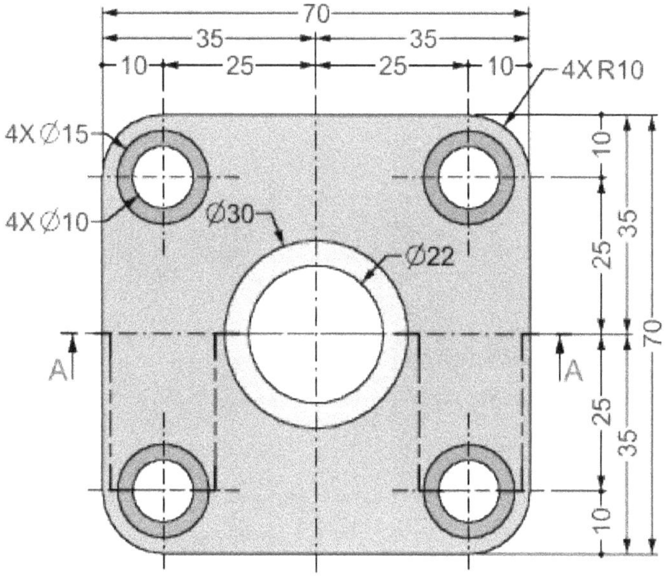

4X Ø15
4X Ø10
Ø30
Ø22
70
35 35
10 25 25 10
4X R10
10
35
25
70
25
35
10
A A

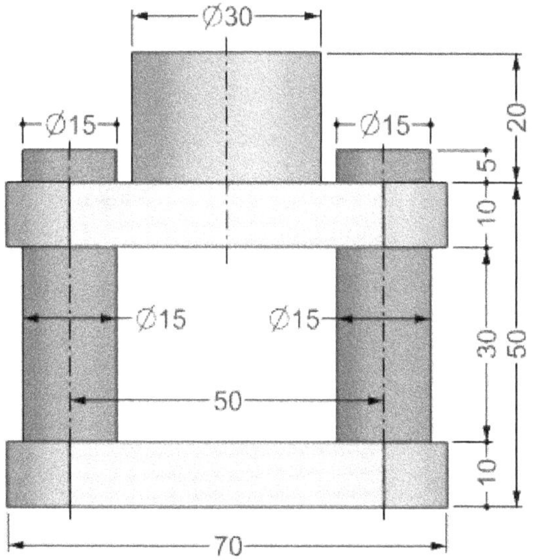

Ø30
Ø15 Ø15
20
5
10
30
50
10
Ø15 Ø15
50
70

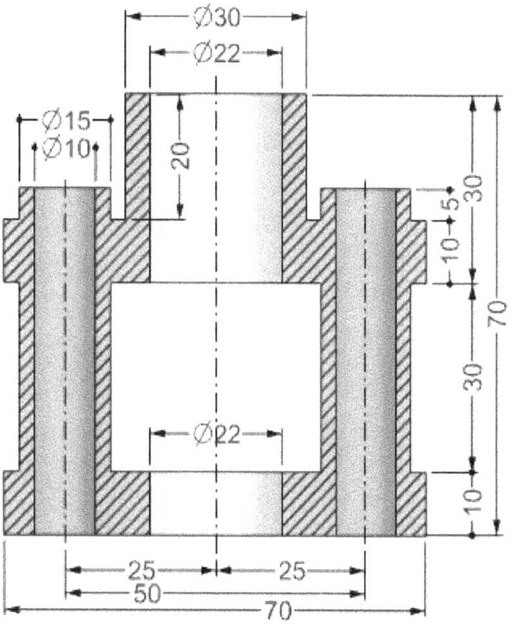

Ø30
Ø22
Ø15
Ø10
20
30
5
10
70
30
10
Ø22
25 25
50
70
SECTION A-A

EX-176

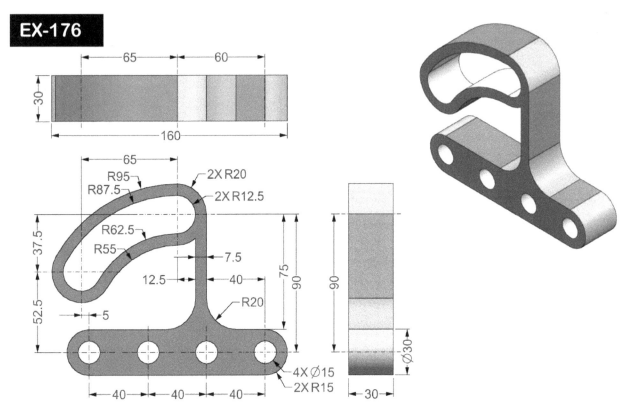

65 | 60

30

160

65

R95
R87.5
2X R20
2X R12.5

R62.5
R55

7.5

37.5

12.5 | 40

75

90

90

52.5

5

R20

Ø30

4X Ø15
2X R15

40 | 40 | 40

30

EX-177

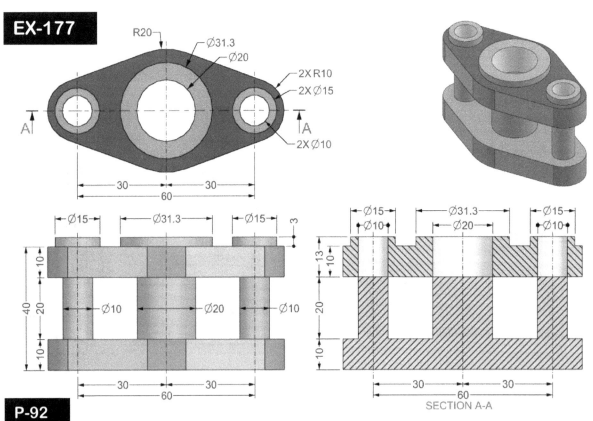

R20
Ø31.3
Ø20

2X R10
2X Ø15

A

A

2X Ø10

30 | 30

60

Ø15 | Ø31.3 | Ø15
3

10

40

20

Ø10

Ø20

Ø10

10

30 | 30

60

Ø15 | Ø31.3 | Ø15
Ø10 | Ø20 | Ø10

13
10

20

10

30 | 30

60

SECTION A-A

P-92

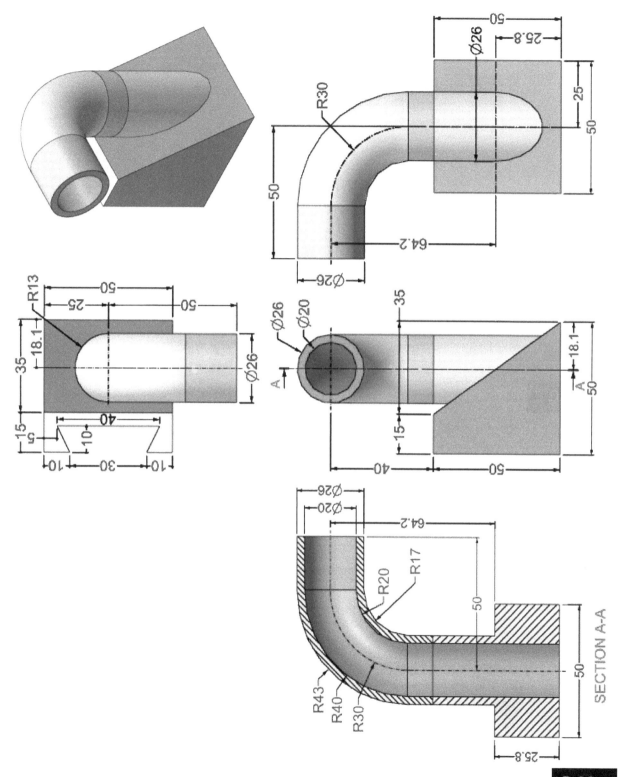

Ø26
Ø20
64.2
R17
R20
50
R43
R40
R30
25.8
50

SECTION A-A

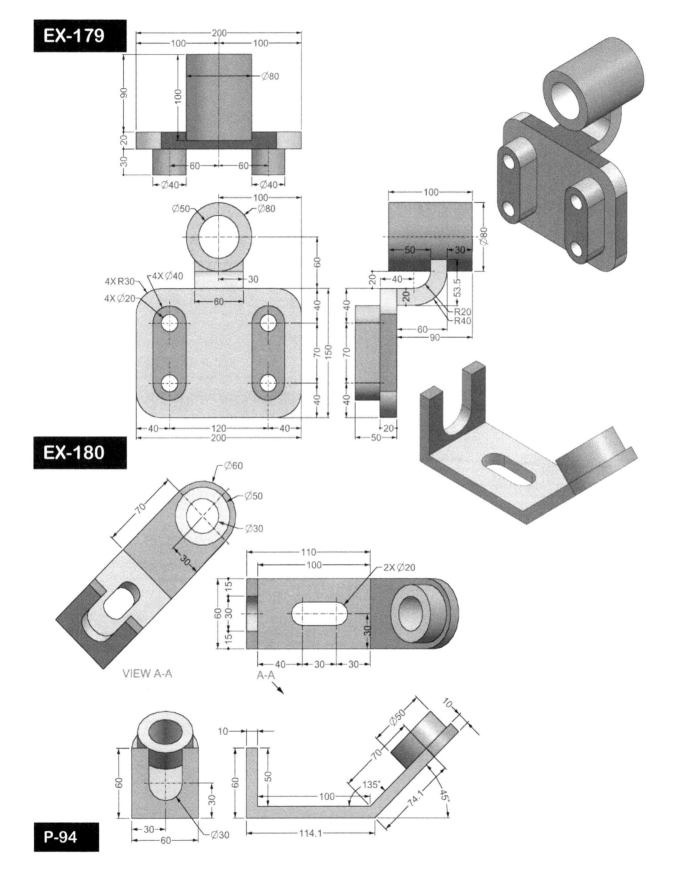

EX-179

Ø80
200
100
100
90
100
20
30
60
60
Ø40
Ø40

Ø50
Ø80
100
60
4X R30
4X Ø40
4X Ø20
30
60
40
70
150
40
40
120
40
200

100
50
30
Ø80
20
40
20
53.5
R20
R40
90
40
70
40
20
50

EX-180

Ø60
70
Ø50
30
Ø30

VIEW A-A

110
100
2X Ø20
15
15
60
30
15
30
40
30
30
A-A

P-94

60
10
30
30
60
Ø30

10
Ø50
70
60
50
135°
100
45°
74.1
114.1

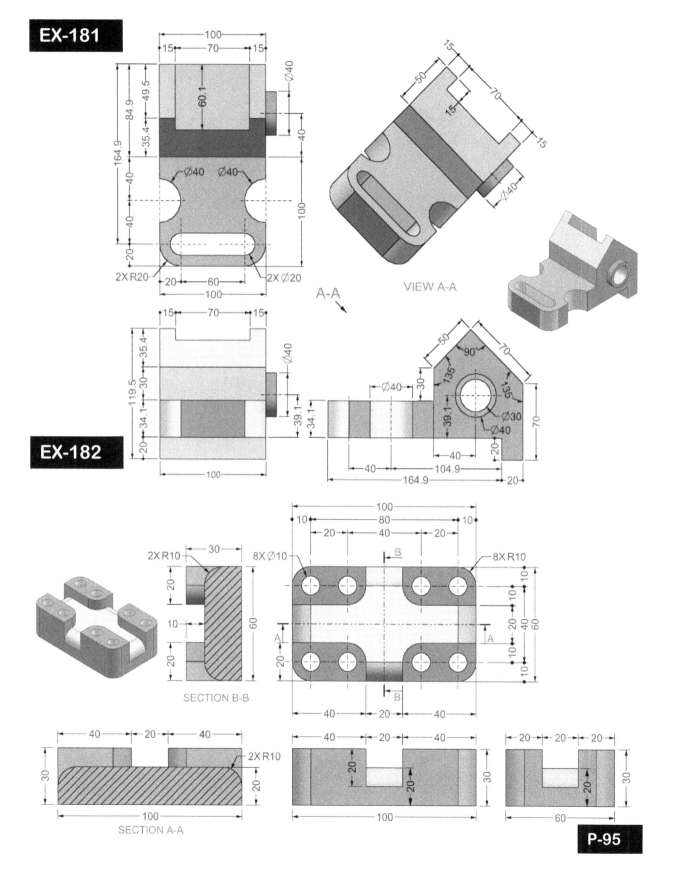

EX-181

EX-182

VIEW A-A

A-A

SECTION B-B

SECTION A-A

P-95

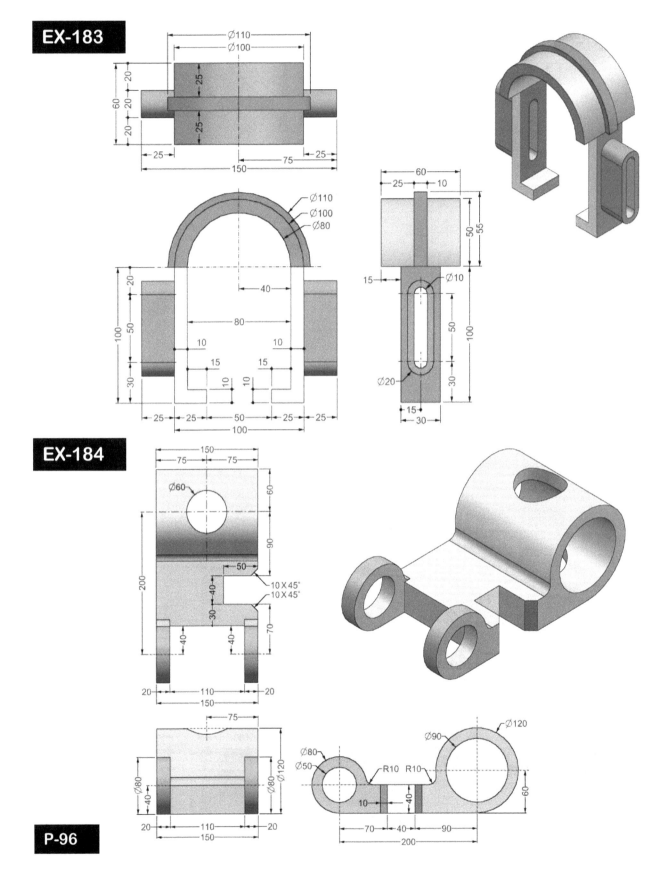

EX-183

EX-184

P-96

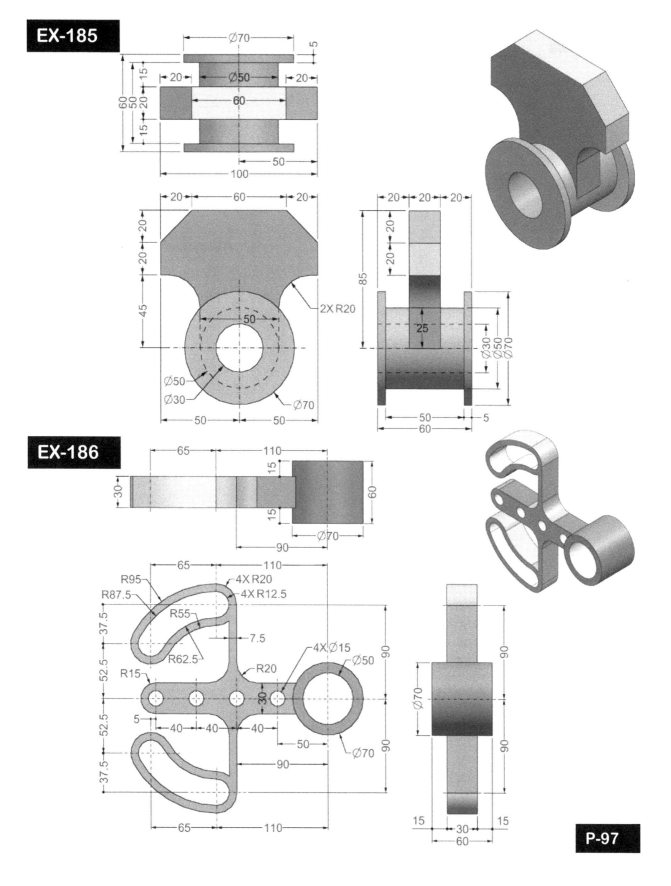

EX-185

EX-186

P-97

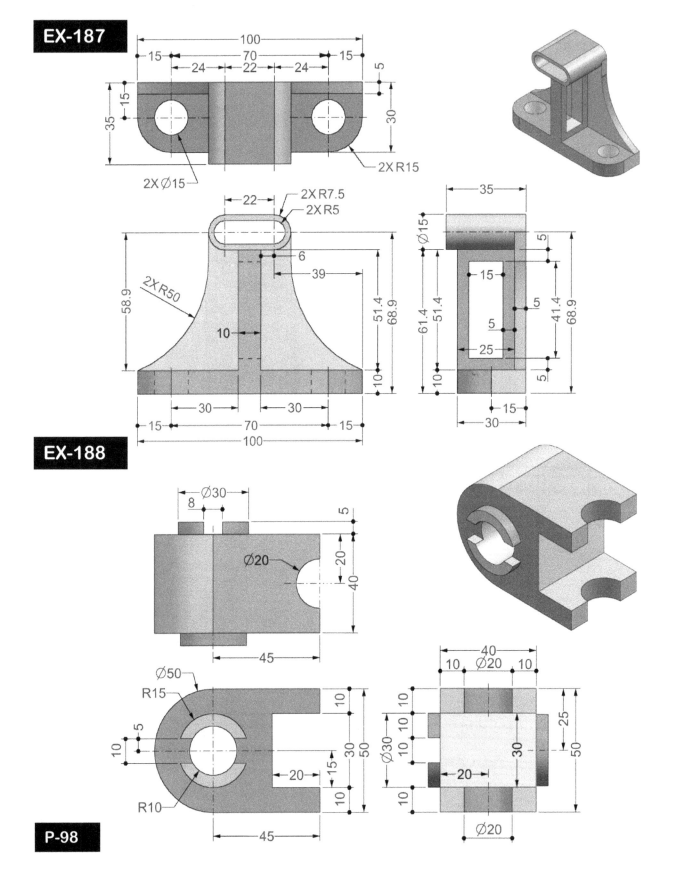

EX-187

2X∅15
2X R15

22
2X R7.5
2X R5
2X R50
58.9
6
39
10
51.4
68.9
30
30
10
15 70 15
100

35
∅15
5
15
61.4
51.4
68.9
5
5
41.4
25
10
5
15
30

EX-188

∅30
8
∅20
5
20
40
45

∅50
R15
5
10
R10
10
30
50
15
20
10
45

40
10 ∅20 10
∅30
10
10
10
10
25
30
50
20
10
∅20

P-98

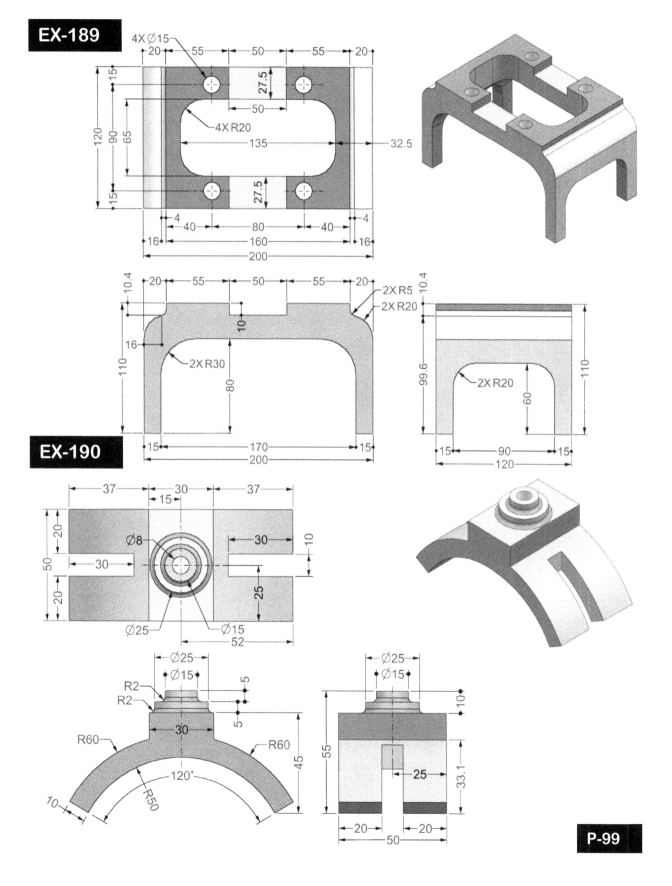

EX-189

EX-190

P-99

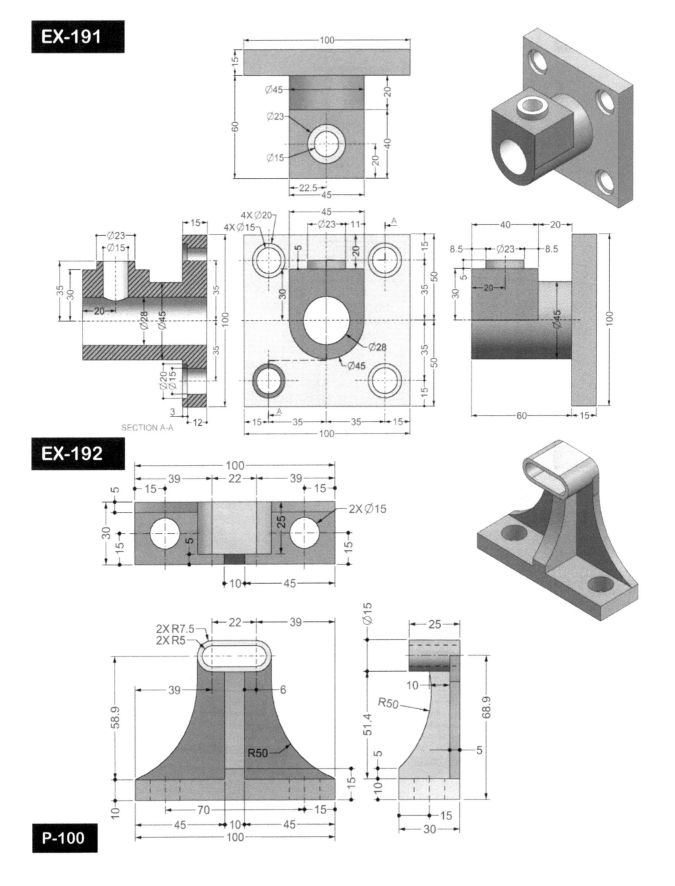

EX-191

Ø45
Ø23
Ø15
100
15
60
20
40
20
22.5
45

Ø23
Ø15
35
30
20
Ø28
Ø45
Ø20
Ø15
3
12
15
SECTION A-A

4X Ø20
4X Ø15
45
Ø23
11
A
5
20
15
50
30
35
50
Ø28
Ø45
35
15
15
35
35
15
100
A
100

40
20
8.5
Ø23
8.5
5
30
20
Ø45
100
60
15

EX-192

100
39
22
39
5
15
15
2X Ø15
30
25
15
5
15
10
45

2X R7.5
2X R5
22
39
Ø15
25
39
6
58.9
R50
51.4
R50
10
68.9
5
15
10
70
15
5
45
10
45
15
30
100

P-100

EX-193

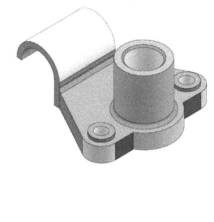

SECTION A-A

2X R10
2X Ø14
2X Ø8
R20
Ø30
15
40
Ø30
Ø20
Ø30
A
Ā
55
30
60
30
10

40
12
10
10
80
60
R2
Ø20
Ø30
1 x 45°
30
10
Ø8
Ø14

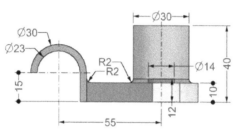

Ø30
Ø23
R2
R2
Ø30
Ø14
15
40
10
12
55

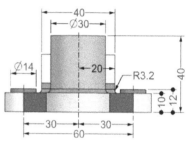

40
Ø30
Ø14
20
R3.2
40
10
12
30
30
60

EX-194

4X Ø20
150
20
110
20
55
40
40
20
R5
15
15
130
30
60
Ø120
40
30
40
70
35
40

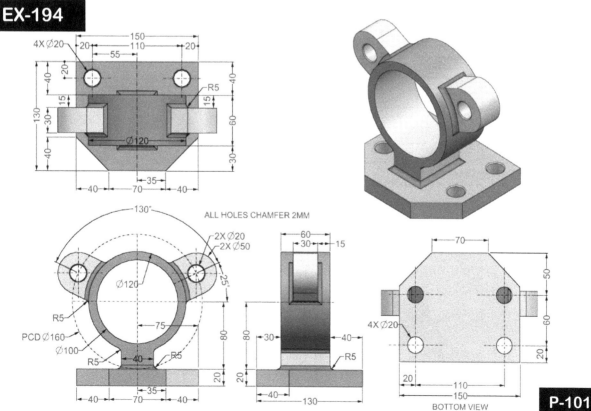

ALL HOLES CHAMFER 2MM

130°
2X Ø20
2X Ø50
25°
Ø120
R5
75
PCD Ø160
80
Ø100
R5
40
R5
20
40
70
35
40

60
30
15
80
30
40
20
R5
40
130

70
50
60
4X Ø20
20
20
110
150
BOTTOM VIEW

P-101

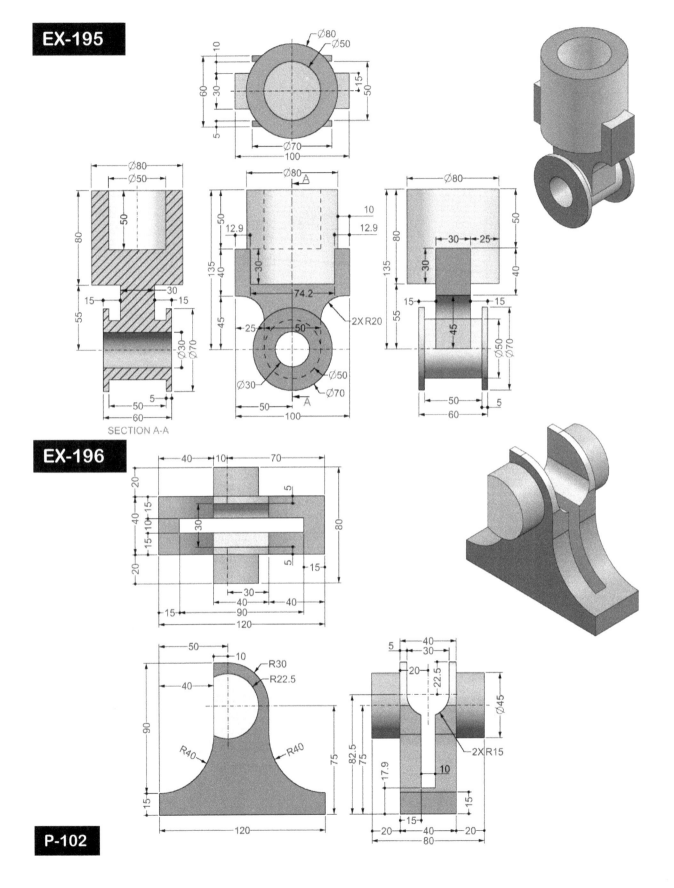

EX-195

Ø80
Ø50
10
60
30
15
50
5
Ø70
100

Ø80
Ø50
80
50
50
15
30
15
55
Ø30
Ø70
5
50
60

SECTION A-A

Ø80
A
10
50
12.9
12.9
135
30
40
74.2
2X R20
45
25
50
Ø30
Ø50
50
Ø70
100
A

Ø80
80
30
25
135
30
40
15
45
15
55
Ø50
Ø70
50
5
60

EX-196

40
10
70
20
5
40
15
10
30
80
15
5
15
30
40
40
20
15
90
120

50
10
R30
R22.5
40
90
R40
R40
75
15
120

5
40
30
20
22.5
Ø45
82.5
75
2X R15
17.9
10
15
15
20
40
20
80

P-102

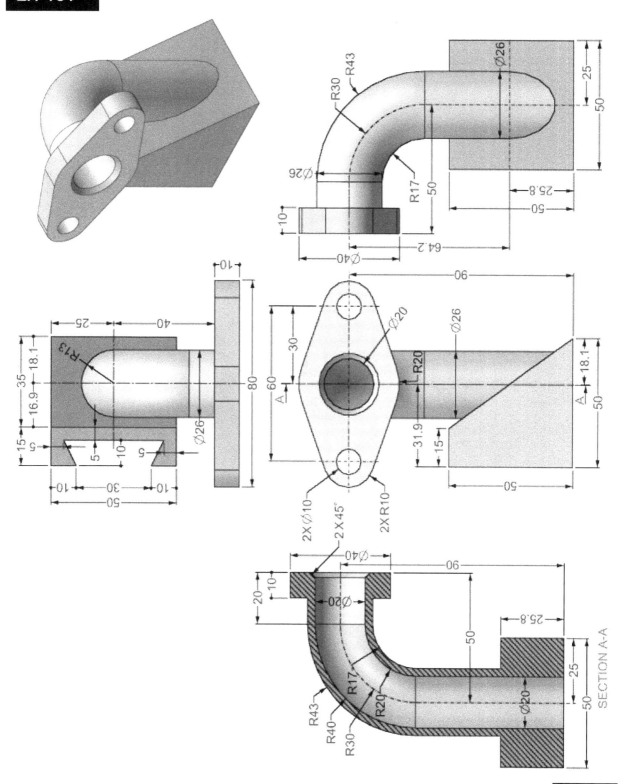

R30
R43
Ø26
Ø26
R17
50
10
Ø40
64.2
25
50
25.8
50

Ø20
90
Ø26
R20
Ø26
30
60
A
A
18.1
50
31.9
15
50

2X Ø10
2 X 45°
2X R10

R13
25
40
10
35
18.1
16.9
15
5
5
10
5
80
Ø26
10
30
10
50

Ø40
90
Ø20
20
10
50
R17
R20
R43
R40
R30
25.8
25
50
Ø20
SECTION A-A

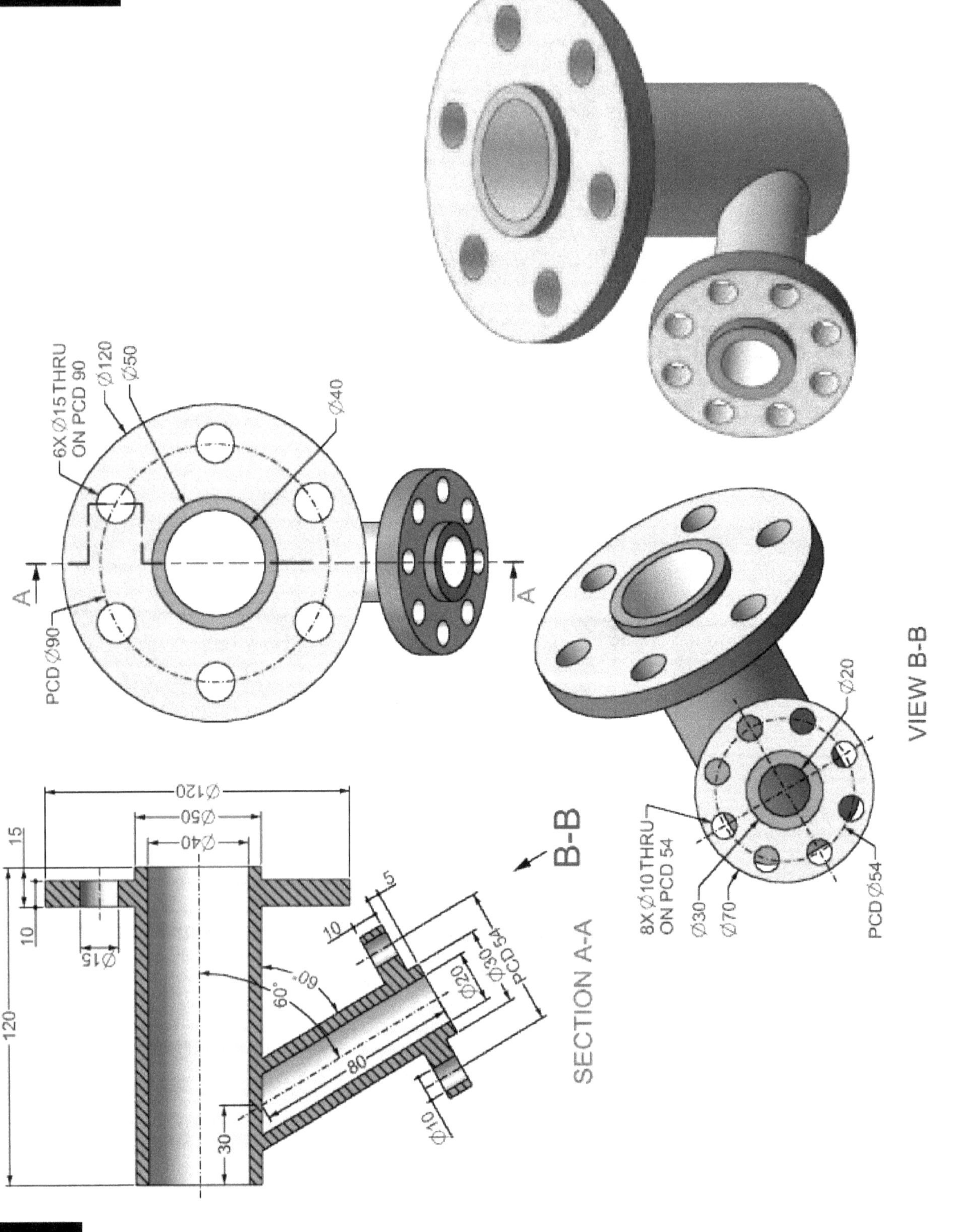

EX-198

6X Ø15 THRU
ON PCD 90
Ø120
Ø50
Ø40

PCD Ø90

A

A

Ø120
Ø50
Ø40
15
10
Ø15
120
60°
60°
30
80
5
10
Ø30
Ø20
PCD 54
Ø10

SECTION A-A

B-B

VIEW B-B

8X Ø10 THRU
ON PCD 54
Ø30
Ø70
Ø20
PCD Ø54

P-104

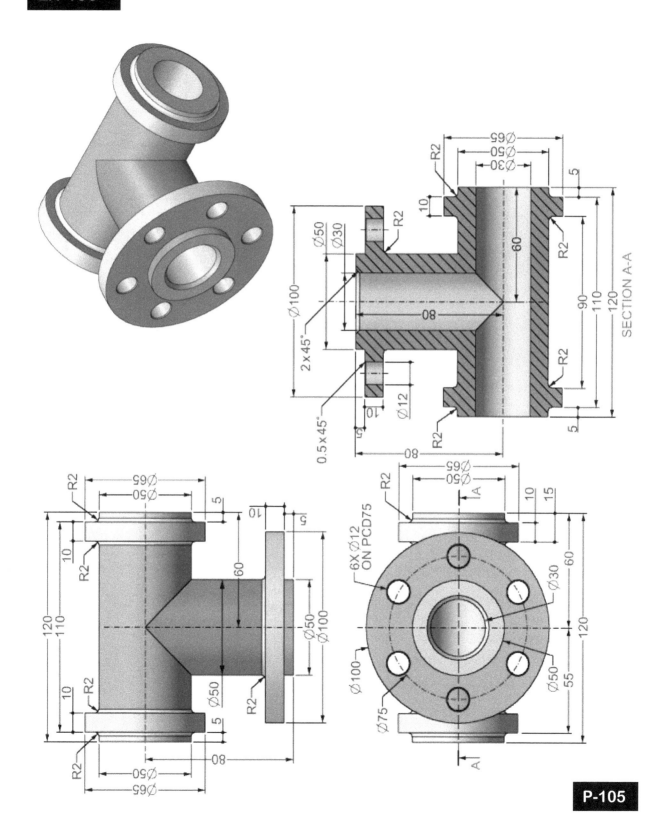

SECTION A-A

6X∅12
ON PCD75

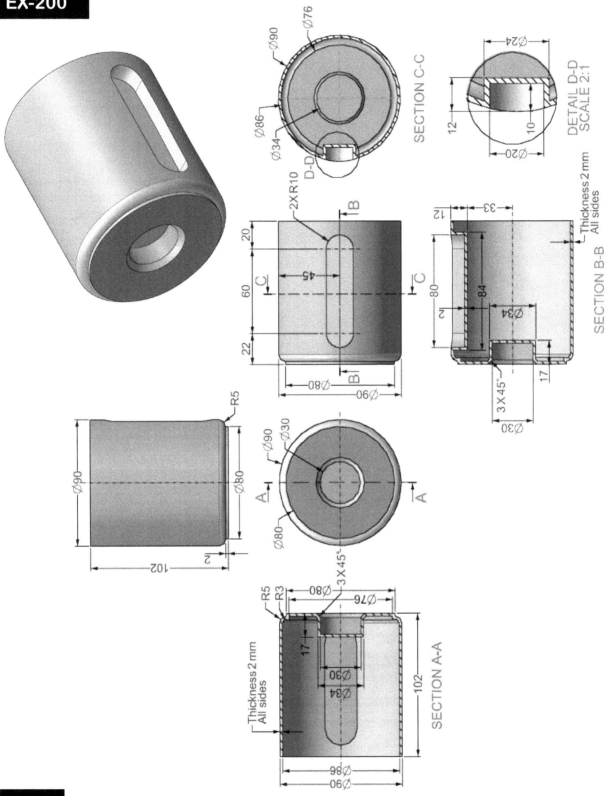

SECTION C-C

Ø90
Ø76
Ø86
Ø34
D-D

DETAIL D-D
SCALE 2:1

Ø24
12
10
Ø20

2×R10
B
20
60
22
C
C
45
Ø80
Ø90
B

Thickness 2 mm
All sides
12
33
80
84
Ø34
2
17
3×45°
Ø30

SECTION B-B

R5
Ø90
Ø80
2
102

Ø90
Ø30
A
A
Ø80

3×45°
R5
R3
Ø80
Ø76
17
Ø30
Ø84
102
Thickness 2 mm
All sides
Ø86
Ø90

SECTION A-A

Other useful books by CADIN360

1. 150 CAD Exercises

2. AutoCAD Exercises

3. CAD Exercises

4. 50+ SolidWorks Exercises

5. SolidWorks 200 Exercises

6. Autodesk Inventor Exercises

7. Catia Exercises

8. Siemens NX Exercises